GAMES WITHOUT LOSERS

LEARNING GAMES AND INDEPENDENT ACTIVITIES FOR ELEMENTARY CLASSROOMS

by
SARAH LIU
and
MARY LOU VITTITOW

ABOUT THIS BOOK . . .

Our goal in developing the games in this book was to make learning in our own classrooms more fun, and to satisfy the needs of children with different levels of experience and proficiency. Our students thoroughly enjoyed the games and showed very rewarding progress. We were so pleased with the success of the games in our classrooms that we felt other teachers might like to try them.

The activities are designed to be uncumbersome and portable. They do not require elaborate display areas but should be easily accessible to the students. Each student then selects activities to meet his individual needs and goes to his own desk or a quiet corner to play and learn. Since most of the games are self-checking, the teacher is free to observe and give assistance when needed.

Many of these learning activities are designed for a child to use alone. This removes the threat of competition for the less capable student. He may use the game to strengthen skills in his own area of deficiency and progress at his own speed without peer pressure or fear of failure. At the other end of the spectrum, the more gifted student may move through the activities much more quickly and participate in the more competitive games, thus avoiding the boredom that often plagues the very capable child. Even in the more competitive games, learning is taking place so no one really loses.

We illustrated each game because we felt it would be helpful to the teacher in making the game. However, do not feel in any way bound to use the same words, facts or dialog shown on our games. We have often used the same game with several different skill levels and even in different content areas. For example, the same game can be used for the simplest addition facts or for division by 2-digit numbers. These games are merely intended to be tools for teaching. The skill needed and level of difficulty may be tailored by each teacher to meet the needs of his or her own class.

We wish to dedicate this book to:

the many volunteers who have helped us
the teachers who have inspired us
our patient and very helpful husbands.

Sarah Liu

Mary Lou Vititow

TABLE OF CONTENTS

CONSONANT CHOO CHOO

SUBJECT AREA: Word Attack and Analysis

SKILL REINFORCED: Beginning Consonants

ADAPTABILITY: Math combinations, number recognition, color recognition

MATERIALS: Poster board, felt pens, construction paper, mystic tape

CONSTRUCTION: Cut poster board into three pieces: 2 end pieces
                       measuring 10½" x 9" and a center piece measuring 10½" x
                       10". Cut 20 4" x 3 3/4" pieces of different colored
                       construction paper for the cars. Fold each piece so
                       it makes an envelope. Attach the three pieces of the
                       board with mystic tape inside and out, making sure the
                       10½" x 10" is in the center. Cut an engine from black
                       paper, and a caboose for Z from red paper. Cut 42
                       black wheels. Glue the engine on the top left of the
                       posterboard. Glue train cars and use mystic tape for
                       the edges. Glue wheels. Write the consonants on the
                       train cars. Link each car to the other with a line as
                       illustrated. Cut 21 2½" x 2" cards. Glue pictures on
                       each one, preferably close to the top of the card, so
                       that, when it is placed in the car, the picture can be
                       seen.

DIRECTIONS FOR   The student matches each card to the beginning consonant
PLAYING: and places it in the right car.

RING AROUND THE PICTURE

SUBJECT AREA: Word Attack and Analysis

SKILL REINFORCED: Consonants

ADAPTABILITY: Math combinations, homonyms, synonyms, antonyms

MATERIALS: Different colors of construction paper, felt pens, old workbooks, scissors, glue, tagboard

CONSTRUCTION: Write three consonants in different colors on top of tagboard. Cut enough pictures that begin with these consonants to fill the board. Then cut rings in colors to correspond with the colors of the consonants.

DIRECTIONS FOR
PLAYING: The student identifies the beginning consonant of each picture. He then places a ring of the same color as that beginning consonant around each picture.

PICK A POCKET

SUBJECT AREA: Word Attack and Analysis

SKILL REINFORCED: Digraphs

ADAPTABILITY: Consonants, blends, math combinations

MATERIALS: Poster board, masking tape, mystic tape, felt pens,
                       scissors

CONSTRUCTION: Cut 2 pieces of poster board 10" x 15". Cut 16 tag-
                       board strips 9" x 1". Space 8 of the strips evenly
                       on each piece of posterboard. Fasten strips with
                       masking tape all across the width of the posterboard,
                       approximately covering the bottom ¼" of each strip.
                       After attaching each strip with masking tape, put
                       masking tape on both sides so the strips are securely
                       fastened. On the left side of each strip, write the
                       consonant digraphs. Use mystic tape to attach the
                       2 pieces of posterboard to make a book. On 16 4" x 2"
                       cards write questions in riddle-like form, for example,
                       "You wear these on your feet," or "The opposite of fat,"
                       to match the consonant digraphs written on the strips.
                       Answers may be written on the back of each card.

DIRECTIONS FOR   The student attempts to guess the answer to the riddle,
PLAYING: then puts the card in the pocket by the right consonant
                       digraph.

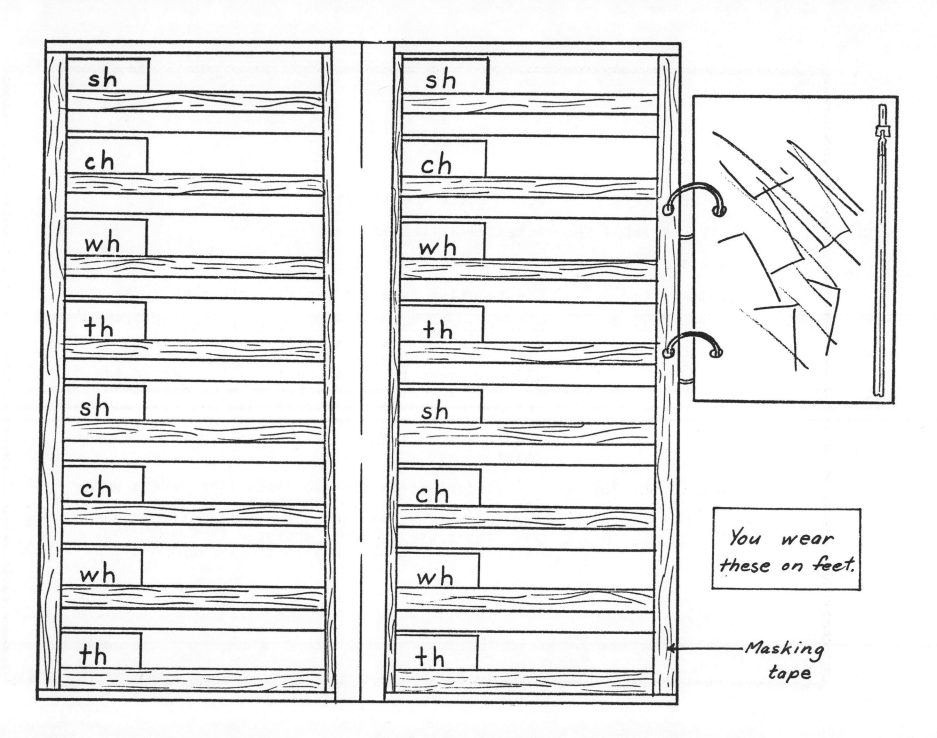

You wear
these on feet.

Masking
tape

TURRETS 'N TANKS

SUBJECT AREA: Word Attack and Analysis

SKILL REINFORCED: Accented Syllables

ADAPTABILITY: Math combinations

MATERIALS: Construction paper, scissors, felt pens

CONSTRUCTION: Draw and cut tanks. Make slits in center of
                     wheels and make a slit where the turret is. Cut
                     discs with tongues to fit the slits in the wheel
                     and also turrets to fit in the slit. Write two
                     syllable words, one syllable on each disc. Put
                     the whole word on the turret. On one side put
                     the accent on the right syllable, on the other put
                     the accent on the wrong syllable. Make an answer
                     sheet.

DIRECTIONS FOR   The student finds the two discs that make a word.
PLAYING: The discs are inserted in the slits. Then he finds
                     the turret that matches the discs, putting the one
                     with the right syllable accented face up. The
                     answers can be checked with the answer sheet.

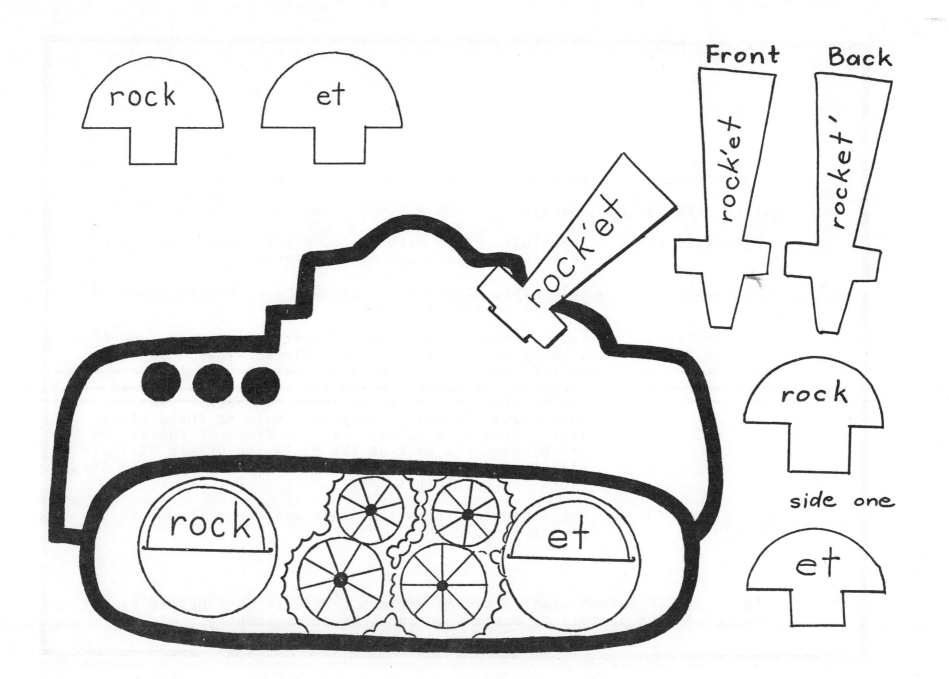

rock

et

Front   Back

rock'et

rocket'

rock'et

rock

et

rock

side one

et

HANG IT ALL

SUBJECT AREA: Word Attack and Analysis

SKILL REINFORCED: Homonyms

ADAPTABILITY: Fractions, basic math facts, capital and lower case
                     letters, phonics, synonyms, antonyms

MATERIALS: Felt pens, velcro*, old gameboard or heavy cardboard,
                     felt or construction paper, scissors

CONSTRUCTION: Cover gameboard with white paper and draw picture of
                     a backyard. Glue velcro for clotheslines. Cut
                     shirts and pants, blouses and skirts from felt or
                     construction paper. Write the items to be matched
                     on the clothes. Glue velcro on the back of the
                     shirts and blouses so they will hold to the clothes
                     line. Also glue velcro onto the front of the shirts
                     and blouses and back of the pants and skirts so those
                     will hold to the tops. Answers may be written on the
                     backs of the clothes.

DIRECTIONS FOR   The student matches the items and hangs the clothes
PLAYING: on the line.

*Sold any place that handles sewing notions. This is an adhesive type
 material used instead of buttons or snaps on dress openings, etc.

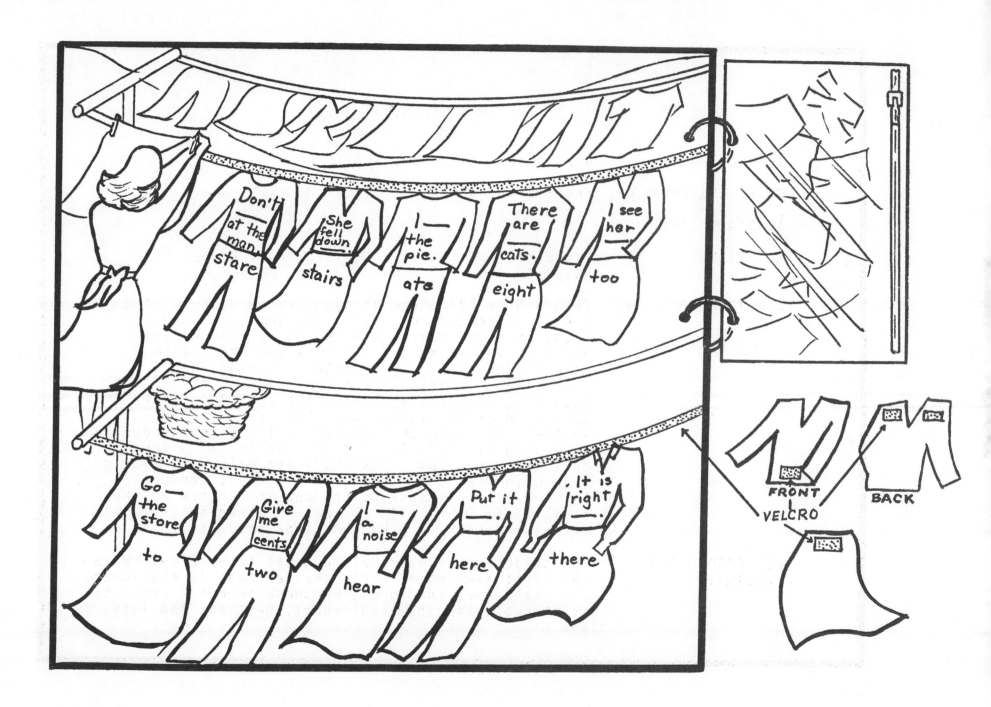

THE VOWEL VENDER

SUBJECT AREA: Word Attack and Analysis

SKILL REINFORCED: Short vowel sounds

ADAPTABILITY:

MATERIALS: Tagboard, felt pens, compass, brads, ruler
                    scissors

CONSTRUCTION: Fold a 9" x 12" piece of tagboard in half to make
                    a 6" x 9" rectangle. Cut 3 windows, 3/4" square
                    each, in the center. The two outer windows are
                    3¼" from the edges and 2½" from top and bottom.
                    Make 2 circles 2½" in diameter. Divide into 8
                    equal segments and write a consonant in each
                    section. Attach the wheels with a brad onto the
                    back fold of the tagboard--1 3/4" from the edge,
                    so that the consonants appear in the outer windows.
                    Make a vowel strip 6¼" x 3/4". Write the 5 vowels
                    on the strip. Cut slits above and below the middle
                    window so that the strip will fit. Cut strips
                    1½" x 3/4" and staple to the top and bottom of the
                    strip so it won't slip through. Either paste decals
                    or paint design to make game look attractive.

DIRECTIONS FOR   The student chooses vowel he wants to work on, turns
PLAYING: the right hand wheel while the left one is stationary
                    and sounds out the words, nonsense or not. After he
                    is through with the right wheel, he turns the left
                    one.

12.

CLOWNING WITH COLOR COMPOUNDS

SUBJECT AREA: Word Attack and Analysis

SKILLS REINFORCED: Compound Words and Color Discrimination

ADAPTABILITY: Any matching activity

MATERIALS: Scissors, posterboard, magnetic strip or velcro*,
                       felt pens, construction paper

CONSTRUCTION: Draw picture of a clown with balloons on poster-
                       board as illustrated. Glue velcro or a piece
                       of magnetic strip on each balloon. Write the
                       first half of the compound word on the top half
                       of the balloon. Cut balloon halves from construc-
                       tion paper to match the color words. Write the
                       second half of the compound word on the balloon
                       halves. On the back of each colored balloon half
                       glue velcro or magnetic strip. Compound words
                       that could be used are: orangeade, blackbird,
                       bluejay, whitecap, redhead, Yellowstone, greenhouse.

DIRECTIONS FOR   The student will match colored balloons to make
PLAYING: compound words.

*Sold any place that handles sewing notions. This is an adhesive type
 material used instead of buttons or snaps on dress openings, etc.

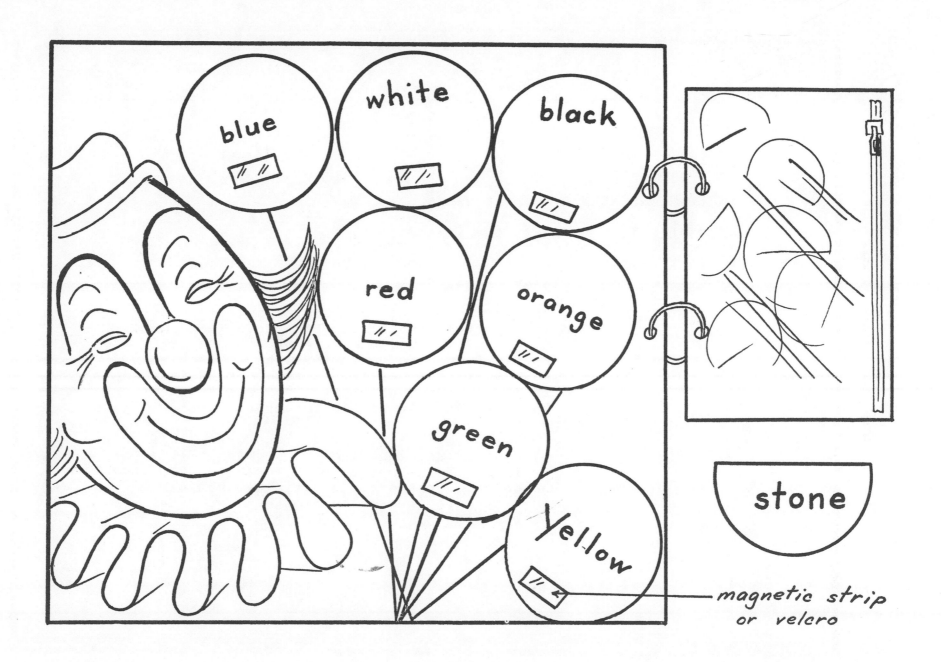

blue

white

black

red

orange

green

Yellow

stone

magnetic strip
or velcro

14.

DIAL-A-RHYME

SUBJECT AREA: Word Attack and Analysis

SKILL REINFORCED: Rhyming words

ADAPTABILITY: Math combinations

MATERIALS: Cardboard, tagboard, spinner, felt pens,
                       glue, scissors

CONSTRUCTION: Cut cardboard into 4 identical circles, 4"
                       in diameter, and divide each into 16 segments.
                       On one circle write words in 8 of the segments.
                       Across from each of those eight write the
                       rhyming words. Cut the other circles into
                       segments. On each segment write words that
                       rhyme with the words on the wheel.

DIRECTIONS FOR   Two can play. Place cards face down. One
PLAYING: student spins, then draws a segment. If it
                       rhymes with the words the spinner pointed to,
                       he gets to keep it. If not, the segment
                       goes back to the bottom of the pile. The
                       player with the most segments wins.

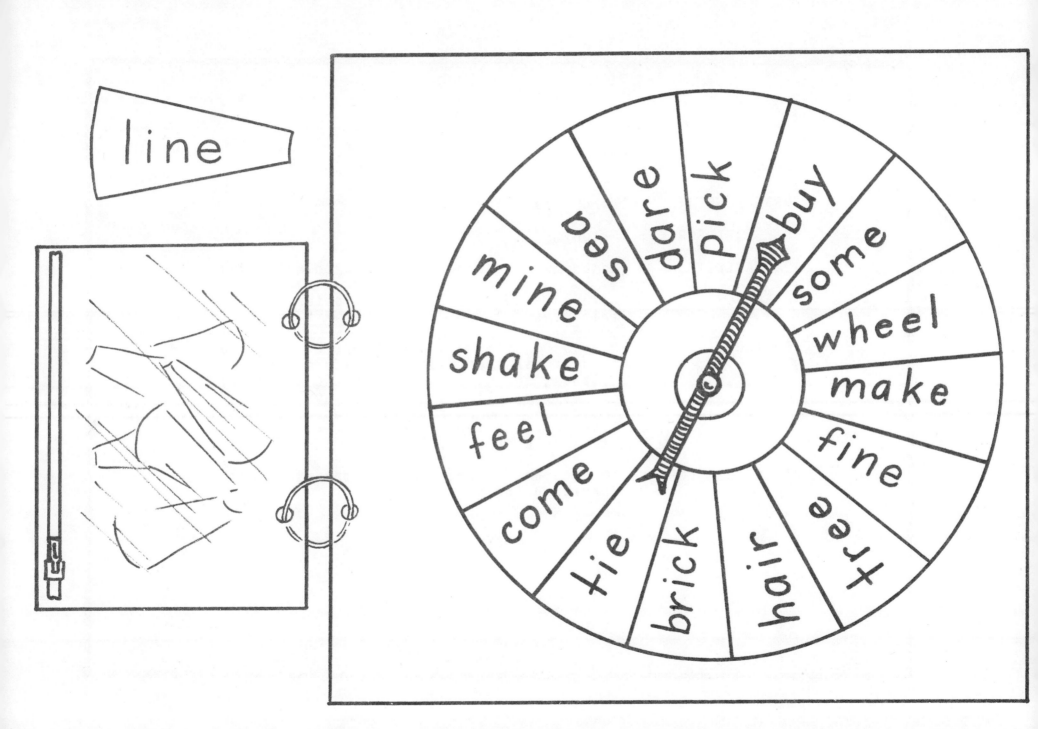

line

sea dare pick buy some wheel make fine tree hair brick tie come feel shake mine

RATS! WHERE ARE THEIR EARS?

SUBJECT AREA: Word Attack and Analysis

SKILL REINFORCED: Antonyms

ADAPTABILITY: Homonyms, synonyms, or any matching activity

MATERIALS: Colored construction paper, posterboard, felt pens

CONSTRUCTION: Make as many mice as desired (see illustration). Make two heads for each mouse, slitting the upper one where the ears would normally be. The other head should remain intact. Cut a pair of ears for each mouse, leaving a tab for insertion. Write matching items on each pair.

DIRECTIONS FOR
PLAYING: The student inserts ears on the mice matching corresponding items.

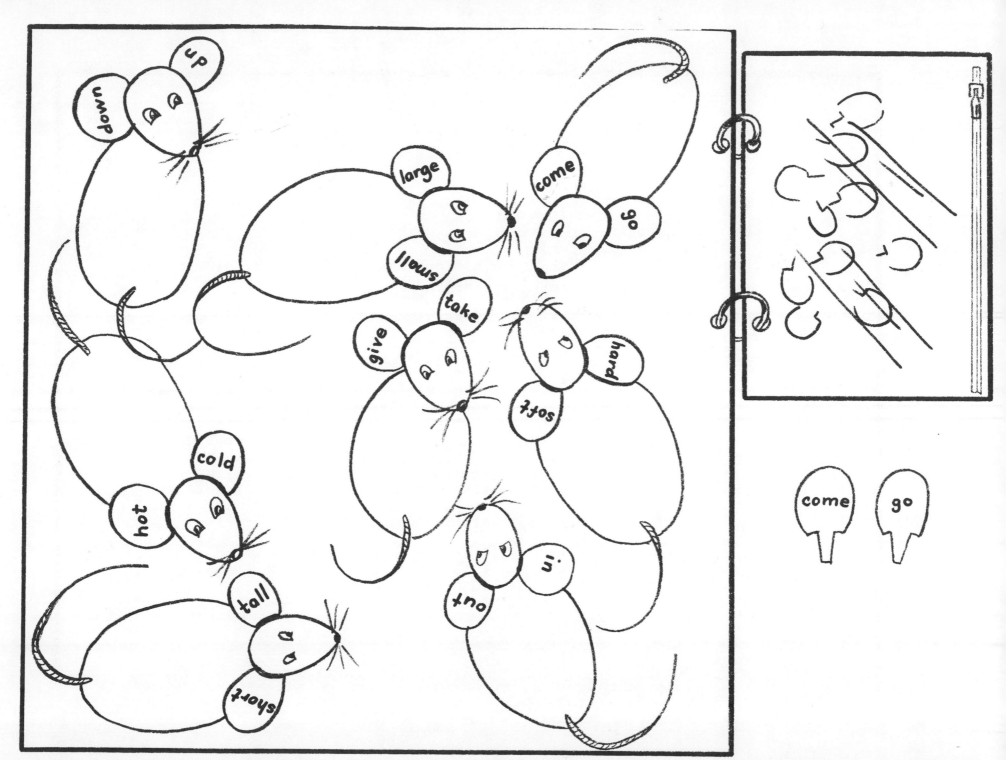

MATCH THE FLAGS

SUBJECT AREA: Word Attack and Analysis

SKILL REINFORCED: Contractions

ADAPTABILITY: Math combinations, parts of speech, map
                       symbols, synonyms, homonyms, antonyms

MATERIALS: Posterboard, paper clips, construction
                       paper, tagboard, felt pens

CONSTRUCTION: Make a ship with 2 pieces of yarn on the
                       sides of the ship joining on the top to form
                       a triangle. Cut decorative flags--two of one
                       size and two of a slightly smaller size for
                       each flag. Glue the 2 larger flags together
                       on the sides only, leaving the bottom side
                       open so that a paper clip can be inserted
                       between the two. Glue these double flags
                       to the posterboard. On each pair of smaller
                       flags write matching items. Answer sheet with
                       correct matches may be included.

DIRECTIONS FOR   The student chooses matching flags and slips
PLAYING: them under the paper clips on the board.

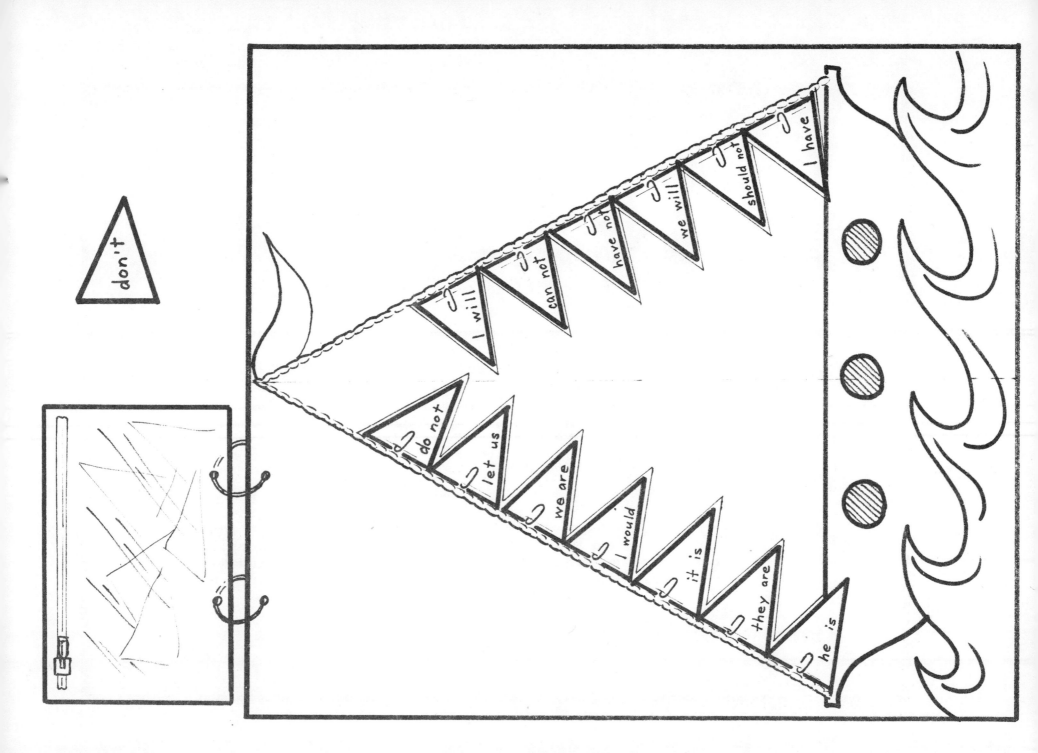

PEEK-A-BOO

SUBJECT AREA: Word Attack and Analysis

SKILL REINFORCED: Accenting syllables

ADAPTABILITY: Question and answer type activities

MATERIALS: Tagboard, exacto knife, felt pens

CONSTRUCTION: Cut tagboard into houselike shape (see illus-
                      tration). Cut evenly spaced windows. On the
                      front, above the windows, write the words to
                      be divided into syllables and accented. On
                      the back, above the windows, write the correct
                      division and accents, reversing the order of
                      the words so that the board can be flipped over
                      to check answers.

DIRECTIONS FOR   The student places his paper under the board
PLAYING: and writes through the cut-out windows the
                      correct division of syllables and accent for the
                      word written above the window. After completing
                      the exercise, he flips the board over and places
                      the back side on top of his paper to check his
                      answers.

FRONT

ACCENTED
SYLLABLES

abandon	appetite	arithmetic
activate	birthday	behave
direction	trapeze	umbrella
postpone	delighted	determine

FRONT

BACK

a rith'me tic	ap'pe tite	a ban'don
be have'	birth'day	ac'ti vate
um brel'la	tra peze'	di rec'tion
de ter'mine	de light'ed	post pone'

BACK

PICK-A-POUCH

SUBJECT AREA: Word Attack and Analysis

SKILL REINFORCED: Long Vowels

ADAPTABILITY: Short vowels, math combinations

MATERIALS: Construction paper, scissors, tagboard, glue,
                     old workbook or pictures, felt pens, heavy
                     cardboard

CONSTRUCTION: Cut 5 kangaroos with one of the vowels written
                     on each of them. Put a picture on each kang-
                     aroo, illustrating that vowel. Staple a pocket
                     to each kangaroo. Then cut pictures and glue
                     on cards to fit in pockets of kangaroos.

DIRECTIONS FOR   The student puts the picture in the pocket
PLAYING: of the matching vowel.

SNAKES

SUBJECT AREA: Word Attack and Analysis

SKILL REINFORCED: Beginning consonants

ADAPTABILITY: Math combinations

MATERIALS: Tagboard, construction paper, scissors, felt
                    pens, pictures from old workbooks

CONSTRUCTION: Choose two colors of construction paper.
                    Cut two identical snakes of each color, for
                    instance, cut two red and two grey. On the
                    one red and one grey snake glue pictures
                    filling up the whole snake. Glue the other
                    red and grey snake down on tagboard. Write
                    the beginning consonants of each picture on
                    the snake that is glued on the tagboard,
                    making sure the consonant is written in the
                    identical place where the picture is on the
                    other snake. Do the same on the other snake.
                    Then cut the snakes that have the pictures.

DIRECTIONS FOR   Two can play. Students take the cut up
PLAYING: pieces of one snake and endeavor to match the
                    picture with its beginning consonant. If
                    done correctly, the cut pieces will form an
                    identical snake. The player to complete the
                    snake first wins.

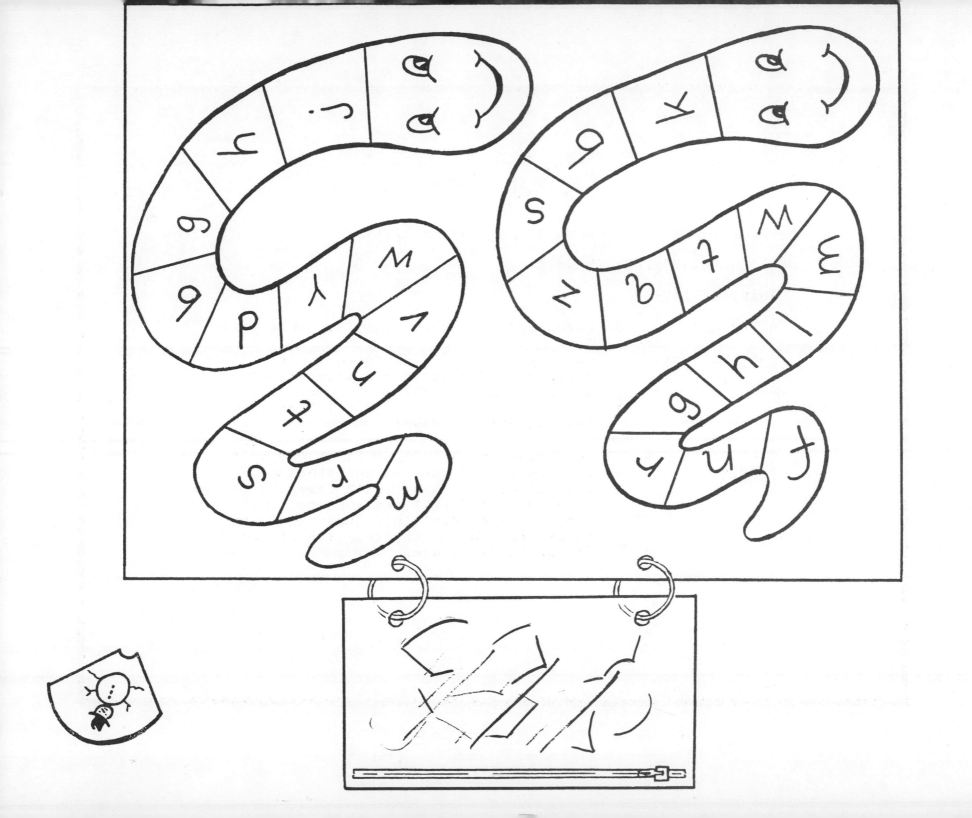

SPIN-A-VOWEL

SUBJECT AREA: Word Attack and Analysis

SKILL REINFORCED: Vowels

ADAPTABILITY:

MATERIALS: Cardboard, spinner, tagboard, felt pens

CONSTRUCTION: Cut cardboard circle, approximately 4" in diameter. Divide into 5 segments and write a vowel on each. On 2 cards of 6½" x 4½" write 3, 4, or 5 letter words, leaving out the vowels.

DIRECTIONS FOR PLAYING: Two students can play. First one spins. The vowel that the spinner stops on is the one he must use. That vowel is filled in on his card--but the word must make sense. If he can't use that vowel, he loses that turn. Whoever gets his card filled in first wins.

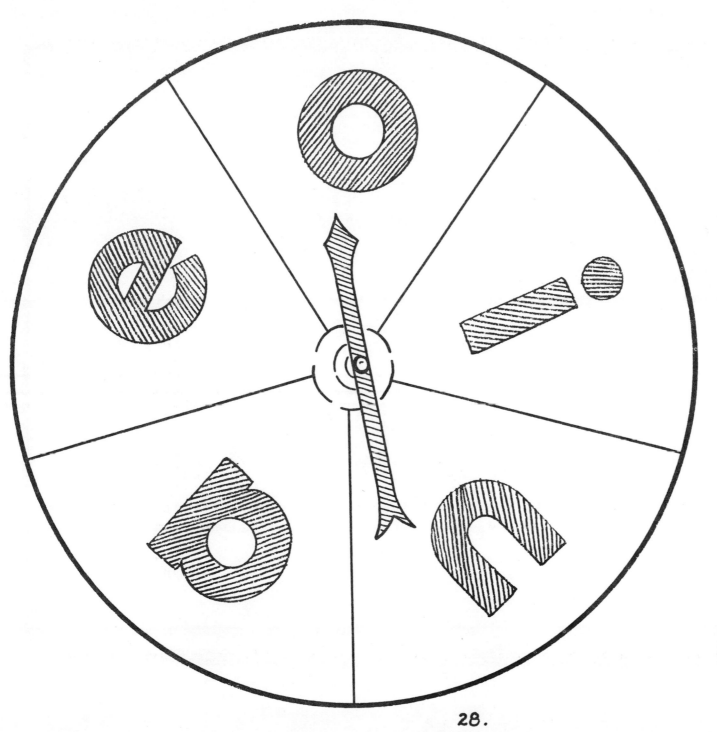

b_t
sp_nd
h_t
d_ck
ch_ck
dr_p
sl_sh

28.

TELL-A-SYNONYM

SUBJECT AREA: Word Attack and Analysis

SKILL REINFORCED: Synonyms

ADAPTABILITY: Homonyms, math combinations

MATERIALS: Construction paper, thumb tacks or brads, scissors, exacto knife, masking tape

CONSTRUCTION: Cut colored construction paper 4½" x 3½" for TV set. Cut a hole 2¼" x 3" for the screen. Cut white construction paper slightly smaller than the TV. Glue colored construction paper on the white. Make a slit on the bottom of the screen. Take a thumb tack with blunted tip and push through the top right side of the TV to represent the dial. Draw 3 circles on the bottom to represent additional dials. Make cards that match the size of the screen with tongues on bottom. Make a circle (with a hole to fit the top dial) to match each screen card. Write the names of TV shows on the screen cards and synonymous ones on the dial, e.g. Gunsmoke and Pistol Fumes. Other titles and synonyms might include "Valley of the Dinosaurs"-- Vale of the Prehistoric Animals; "Hollywood Squares"-- California Rectangles, etc.

DIRECTIONS FOR PLAYING: The student matches the TV shows with its synonyms.

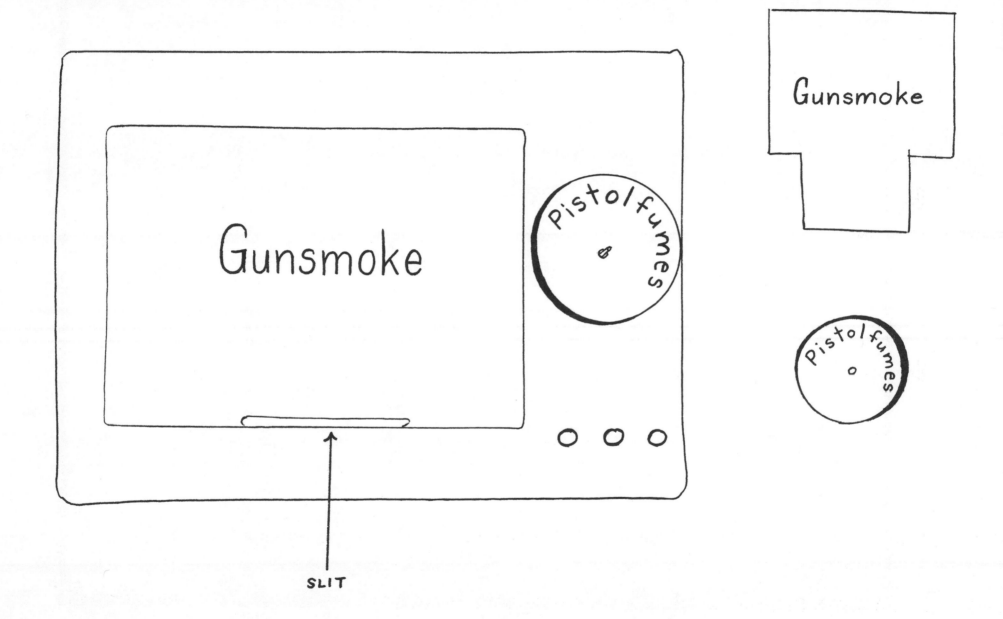

Gunsmoke

Pistolfumes

SLIT

Gunsmoke

Pistolfumes

CATCH-A-BLEND

SUBJECT AREA: Word Attack and Analysis

SKILL REINFORCED: Blends

ADAPTABILITY: Math combinations

MATERIALS: Felt pens, construction paper, brads, scissors

CONSTRUCTION: Draw and cut baseball mitt. Make a circle to attach to the middle. Write consonant blend on the circle and corresponding words on the mitt. Attach circle to mitt with brad.

DIRECTIONS FOR
PLAYING: If a few of these are made they can be used in a group. Otherwise, only one can play and another student can check to see if the words are being pronounced correctly.

we

ess

oom

ind

ame

ouse

ossom

en

bl

32.

TELL IT LIKE IT IS

SUBJECT AREA: Word Attack and Analysis

SKILL REINFORCED: Extending Vocabulary

ADAPTABILITY: Possibly numbers if a suitable picture is
                       found

MATERIALS: A large picture, tagboard, construction
                       paper, scissors, paper clips, felt pen

CONSTRUCTION: Glue picture to tagboard. Make an envelope
                       and attach to bottom of tagboard. Make
                       word cards for the objects in the picture.
                       Cut slits next to the objects for which you
                       have word cards and insert paper clips in
                       the slits.

DIRECTIONS FOR   The student matches word card to the object
PLAYING: by placing it under the paper clip.

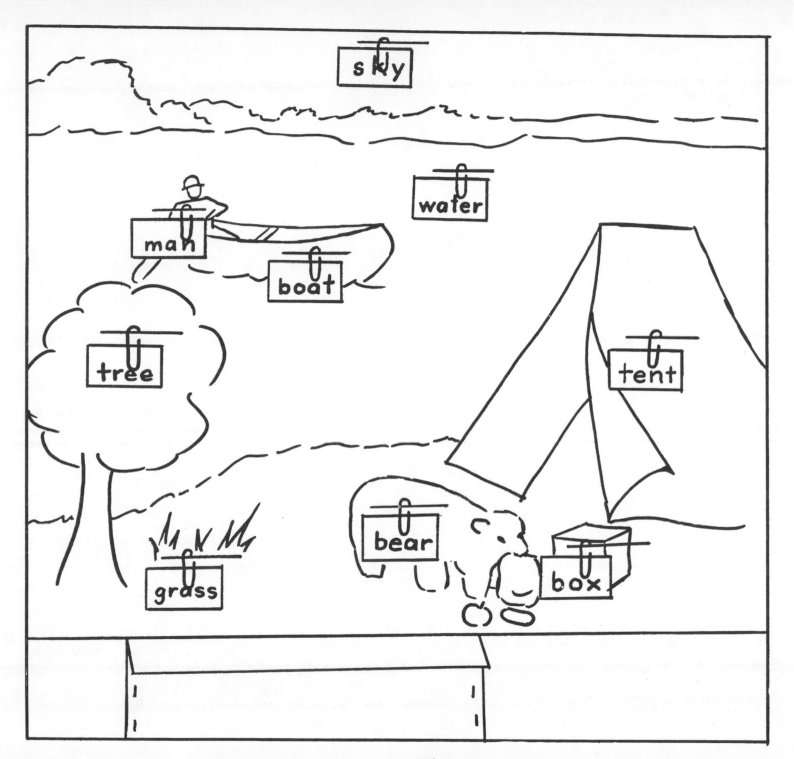

LACE UPS

SUBJECT AREA: Word Attack and Analysis

SKILL REINFORCED: Homonyms

ADAPTABILITY: Fractions, basic math facts, phonics, word recognition,
                     synonyms, antonyms, geometric shapes, map symbols

MATERIALS: Stiff cardboard, 1" wide masking tape, solid color contact
                     paper, plastic-tipped shoe laces (8), compass or any
                     pointed instrument, ruler, plastic acetate, tagboard, felt
                     pens

CONSTRUCTION: Cut a vest from cardboard measuring 10" across and 16" down
                     from the shoulders. Decorate as desired. Cut 2 strips of
                     plastic acetate 13" x 3¼". Place these strips down each
                     side of board, about 1" from top. Use masking tape along
                     both sides (lengthwise) of the acetate to hold it in place.
                     Then use a pointed instrument to punch holes next to the
                     acetate on each side. The first hole is approximately
                     1 3/4" from the top and the 7 succeeding holes are approxi-
                     mately 1¼" apart. After holes are punched, push shoe lace
                     through each hole on just one side and then tie a knot in
                     the shoelace on the underside. Now cut tagboard strip 14"
                     x 2". Write items to be matched on one strip making sure
                     the spacing of the items matches the holes on the vest. On
                     the other strip write the corresponding items in a differ-
                     ent order, again making sure the items are spaced so they
                     match the holes.

DIRECTIONS FOR   The student slides strips under the acetate and then uses
PLAYING: the shoe laces to show the matching items.

sale
rain
sent
rows
nose
write
seem
reel
rode
there

road
reign
rose
sail
scent
seam
right
real
their
knows

HANG IT RIGHT

SUBJECT AREA: Reading Readiness

SKILL REINFORCED: Sequence

ADAPTABILITY: Creative writing

MATERIALS: Pictures in sequence, paper clips, posterboard
                       or manila folder, felt pens, ruler

CONSTRUCTION: Cut pictures to make a story. Mount on 3" x 4"
                       tagboard cards. On a 9" x 12" posterboard or
                       manila folder draw 3½" x 4½" rectangles to
                       represent frames. Punch holes about 1" from
                       top of each frame. Twist paper clip to make
                       hook. Poke through hole. Put numerals in
                       corner of each frame to show the order in which
                       the pictures should go. Cover back of board
                       with contact paper to hide paper clips.

DIRECTIONS FOR   The student puts the pictures in sequential
PLAYING: order and can tell the story to a classmate.

STAR DUST

SUBJECT AREA: Reading Readiness

SKILLS REINFORCED: Counting and Visual Discrimination

ADAPTABILITY: Color recognition

MATERIALS: Poster board, stick-on stars of several colors,
                         felt pens

CONSTRUCTION: Overlap a large circle, square, and triangle (see
                         illustration). Stick the different colored stars
                         on the board at random.

                         Cut approximately 20 cards that measure 7" x 4".
                         Draw a smaller version of the board design on a
                         ditto to fit the 7" x 4" cards. Run the ditto
                         directly onto the tagboard cards. Shade in one or
                         more areas on each card and stick on one colored
                         star. No two cards should be exactly alike. On
                         the back of each card write the answer--the number
                         of those particular colored stars in that shaded
                         area.

DIRECTIONS FOR   The student will count the number of stars of that
PLAYING: particular color shown on his card in the shaded
                         area.

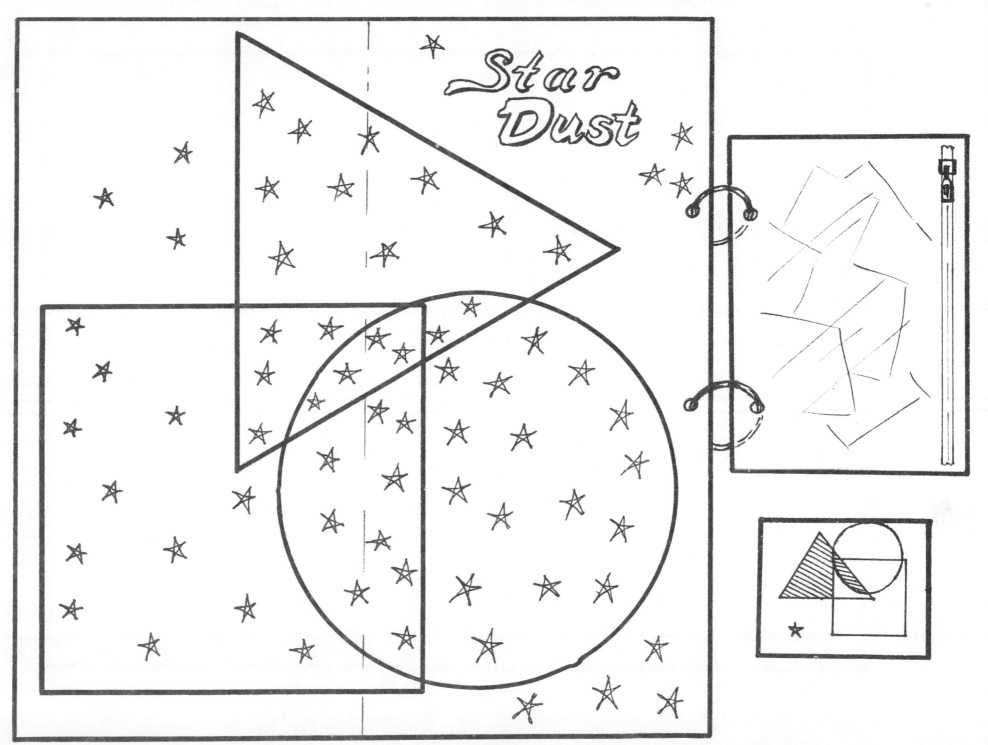

Star Dust

40.

ALTOGETHER, NOW!

SUBJECT AREA: Reading Readiness

SKILL REINFORCED: Story sequence

ADAPTABILITY: Activities that require sequencing

MATERIALS: Felt pens, notebook rings, pictures of three or
                       four stories, tagboard, hole punch

CONSTRUCTION: Glue pictures on 3½" x 5" cards. Cut 2 pieces
                       of tagboard 12" x 5" for the covers. The first
                       picture of each story should be on top. Punch
                       holes in the cards and attach them to the covers.
                       The second picture of each story should be
                       attached next, but in a different order than the
                       first set of cards. The next set of cards should
                       also be in an order different from the other two
                       sets.

DIRECTIONS FOR   The student attempts to find the pictures that
PLAYING: go together and tells about them.

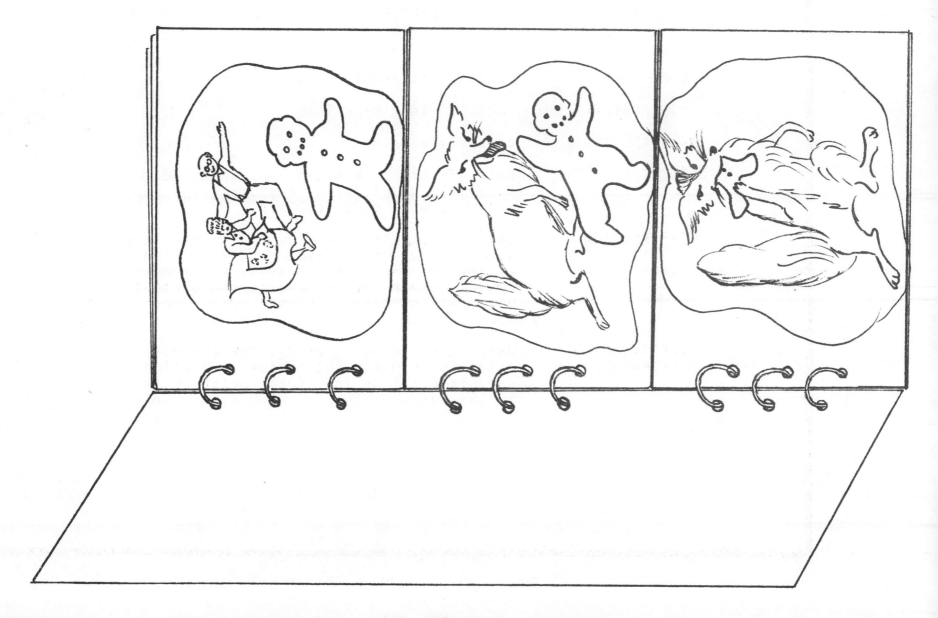

FEELY FUN

SUBJECT AREA: Reading Readiness

SKILL REINFORCED: Tactile discrimination

ADAPTABILITY: Creative writing

MATERIALS: Pair of child's glasses, masking tape, glue,
                       materials of different texture (e.g. sand-
                       paper, towel, corduroy, etc.)

CONSTRUCTION: Cut the materials neatly, making sure there
                       are 2 pieces of the same texture. Glue one
                       of the pair in a box, leaving a space be-
                       tween. Cover the outside of the glasses
                       with masking tape so player cannot see
                       through.

DIRECTIONS FOR   Wearing the taped glasses, the student
PLAYING: attempts to match the textures, putting
                       each material on top of the matching one
                       in the box.

44.

HOOKED ON COLORS

SUBJECT AREA: Reading Readiness

SKILL REINFORCED: Color discrimination

ADAPTABILITY: Comparison of adjectives, alphabetizing, number ordering

MATERIALS: Large piece of heavy cardboard, plywood, or the back of a sample wallpaper holder, hooks or brads, paint sample cards, approximately 4 or 5 of the same color in varying shades (for color discrimination game), tagboard, hole punch, felt pens

CONSTRUCTION: Drill holes in cardboard spacing them far enough apart for the cards. If brads are used, insert one part of the brad through cardboard and bend for a hook. A stand can be made for the board or it can be propped against a wall. For games other than color discrimination, cut tagboard into cards measuring 3½" x 2" and write on them.

DIRECTIONS FOR PLAYING: The student puts the cards on the hooks, all cards of the same color in one row, arranging them from lightest to darkest.

45.

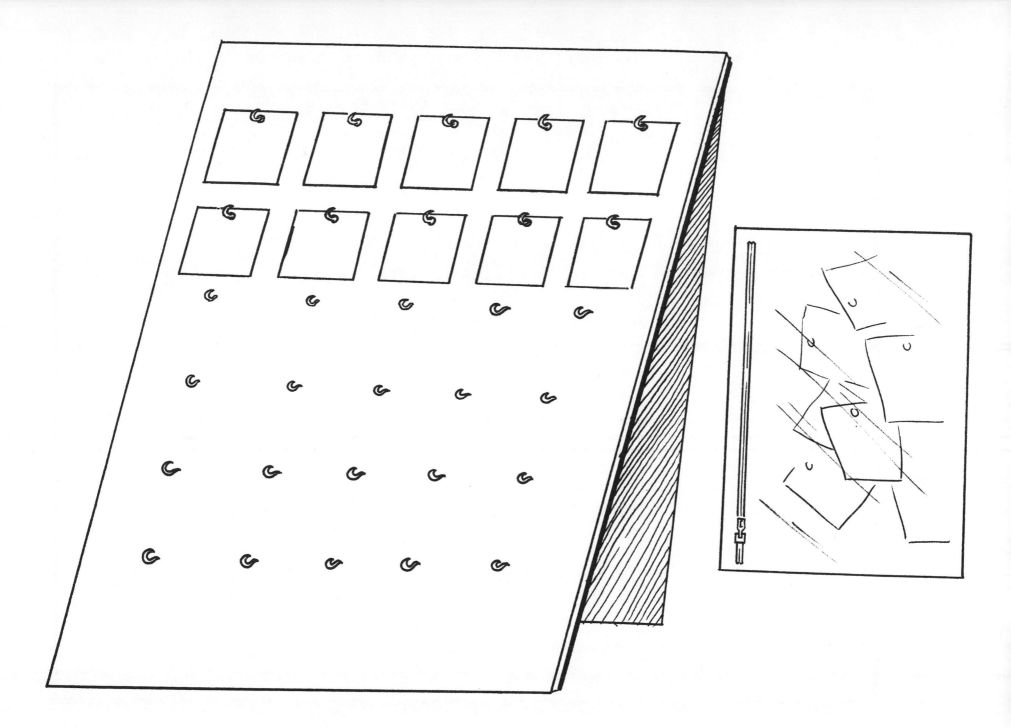

46.

MAILING MAIN IDEAS

SUBJECT AREA: Language comprehension

SKILL REINFORCED: Identifying main ideas

ADAPTABILITY: Addition, subtraction, multiplication

MATERIALS: Gameboard or heavy cardboard, construction paper, scissors, magnetic strip, glue

CONSTRUCTION: Cover gameboard with white construction paper. Cut a mailman and mailbox of contrasting construction paper. Make the mailbox 2 thicknesses so it can be slit. Put a strap on the mailman but do not attach a mailbag. On 3" x 3" pieces of different colored construction paper, type stories. The 3" x 3" pieces represent the mailbags. On the end of the strap, glue a piece of magnetic strip. Also glue a piece on the back of each mailbag. On 1½" x 3" pieces of construction paper type at least 3 choices of main ideas for each story on the mailbags. Cards should look like envelopes and correspond in color to the mailbags.

DIRECTIONS FOR   The student puts a colored mailbag on the mailman;
PLAYING: then makes a choice of main ideas from the matching envelopes and places that envelope in the mailbox.

47.

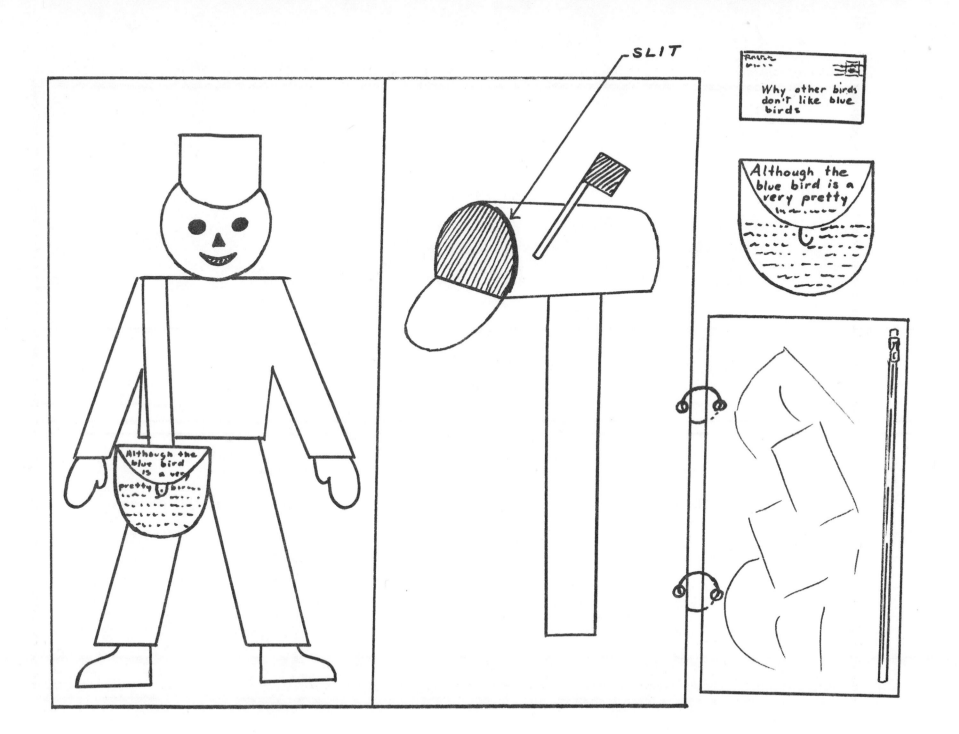

SLIT

Why other birds
don't like blue
birds

Although the
blue bird is a
very pretty

Although the
blue bird
is a very
pretty bird

48.

BEGINNING THE BASICS

SUBJECT AREA: Language comprehension

SKILL REINFORCED: Vocabulary development

ADAPTABILITY:

MATERIALS: Posterboard, pictures unfamiliar to the
                       children, tagboard, paper clips or brads
                       felt pens

CONSTRUCTION: Either glue pictures or draw cartoon-type
                       illustrations. Attach hooks under each picture,
                       with paper clips or brads. On 1½" x 3" cards
                       print words and sentences from the basal reader
                       appropriate for each illustration.

DIRECTIONS FOR   The student reads each card and places it under
PLAYING: the appropriate illustration.

c
Julie pulls Puff and Bob.

c
Bob and Puff fall out.

SENTENCE SCRAMBLE

SUBJECT AREA: Language comprehension

SKILL REINFORCED: Putting words in sequence

ADAPTABILITY: Sentence sequence, or any other sequencing
                        activity

MATERIALS: Felt pens, tagboard, exacto knife, notebook
                        rings or mystic tape

CONSTRUCTION: Cut two buses (one for the cover). On one
                        cut slits in the windows. Cut word cards
                        that make a sentence. Make a tongue on
                        each card (see illustration) to fit in the
                        slit. With mystic tape or notebook rings
                        join the two buses to make a book.

DIRECTIONS FOR   The student puts the words in order to
PLAYING: make a sentence.

like we the

SKYSCRAPING WITH STORY SEQUENCE

SUBJECT AREA: Language comprehension

SKILL REINFORCED: Story sequence

ADAPTABILITY: Activities requiring sequencing

MATERIALS: Tagboard, felt pens, mystic tape, scissors

CONSTRUCTION: Draw 2 skyscrapers--one for the cover, one
                     for the game itself. On one, make slits
                     on opposite sides (see illustration). Write
                     parts of a story on strips that will fit in
                     the slits. On the back of each strip, write
                     a numeral corresponding to the order in the
                     story.

DIRECTIONS FOR   The student will take the strips and endeavor
PLAYING: to put the story in the correct sequence.

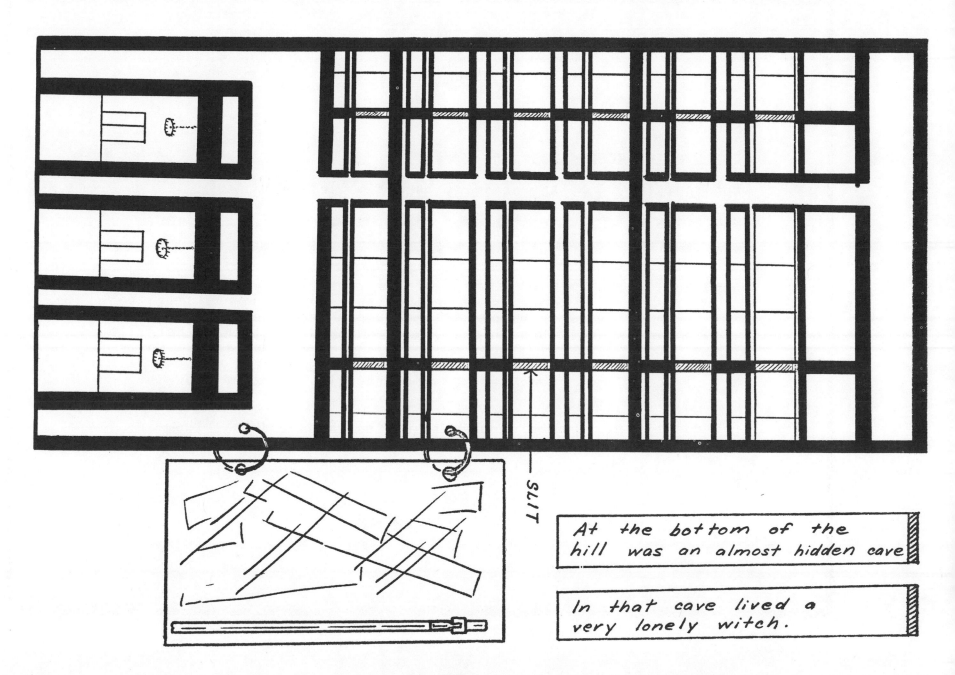

SLIT

At the bottom of the
hill was an almost hidden cave

In that cave lived a
very lonely witch.

54.

SEQUENCE ON THE SHIP

SUBJECT AREA: Spelling

SKILL REINFORCED: Dictionary skills

ADAPTABILITY: Any activity requiring sequencing

MATERIALS: Construction paper, posterboard, felt pens, tagboard, paper clips or brads, mystic tape, hole punch, contact paper

CONSTRUCTION: Make a ship (see illustration) with four masts. Poke holes on the masts where the hooks are to be placed. Twist paper clip and push one end through hole. The other side of the paper clip will need to be held with masking tape. Cover the back of the board with contact paper. Make word cards in sequential order to fit on the hooks.

DIRECTIONS FOR
PLAYING: The student takes the cards and puts them in alphabetical order.

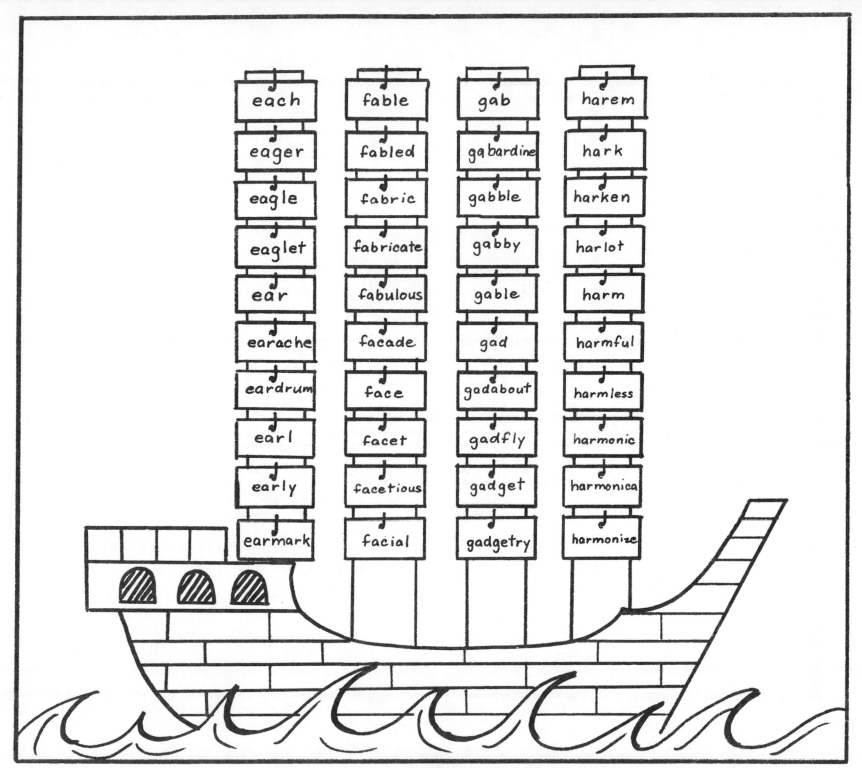

STORY BONANZA

SUBJECT AREA: WRITING

SKILL REINFORCED: Creative writing

ADAPTABILITY:

MATERIALS: Felt pens, colored posterboard, brads, compass, ruler
                         decals or pictures from old workbooks

CONSTRUCTION: Cut posterboard to 18" x 9". Cut 3 windows. 2 outer
                         windows should measure 2½" x 1". Cut these 2 windows
                         3½" from the outer edge and 4" from the top and bot-
                         tom. The middle window measures 2" x 1¼". Cut it 8"
                         from the outer edges, 3¼" from the top and 4½" from
                         the bottom. Cut 3 circles from tagboard dividing
                         them into 8 equal segments. On one circle write 8
                         "who's"; on the second circle write 8 "when's"; on
                         the third circle write eight "where's"--for example,
                         "the pirate, 100 years ago, outer space." Attach the
                         "who" circle on the left side 2½" from the edge,
                         4½" from the top. The "when" circle should be
                         attached 2 3/4" from the bottom and 9¼" from the left
                         side. The third circle should be attached on the
                         right 2½" from the edge and 4½" from the bottom.

DIRECTIONS FOR   The student spins all three wheels to find a story
PLAYING: starter.

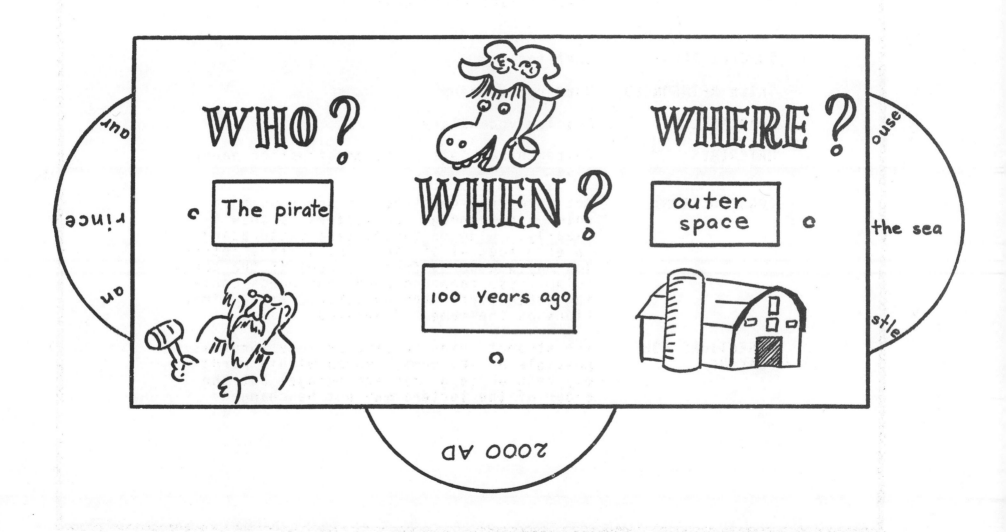

WILLIE THE WORDY WORM

SUBJECT AREA: Spelling

SKILL REINFORCED: Word recognition

ADAPTABILITY: Reading vocabulary

MATERIALS: Posterboard, felt pens, construction paper, glue

CONSTRUCTION: Cut worm from construction paper using a color light enough for letters to show clearly. Glue on contrasting posterboard. In each segment of the worm, write a letter. You may use words from any area of the curriculum. Use compound words and words containing other words when possible. Write directions on the game, if desired.

DIRECTIONS FOR PLAYING: The student tries to find as many words as possible on the worm. Words within words may be used (e.g. man and manage) but the order of the letters may not be changed.

Willie
the word worm

How many words can you find? You may use a word within a word but you may not change the order of the letters.

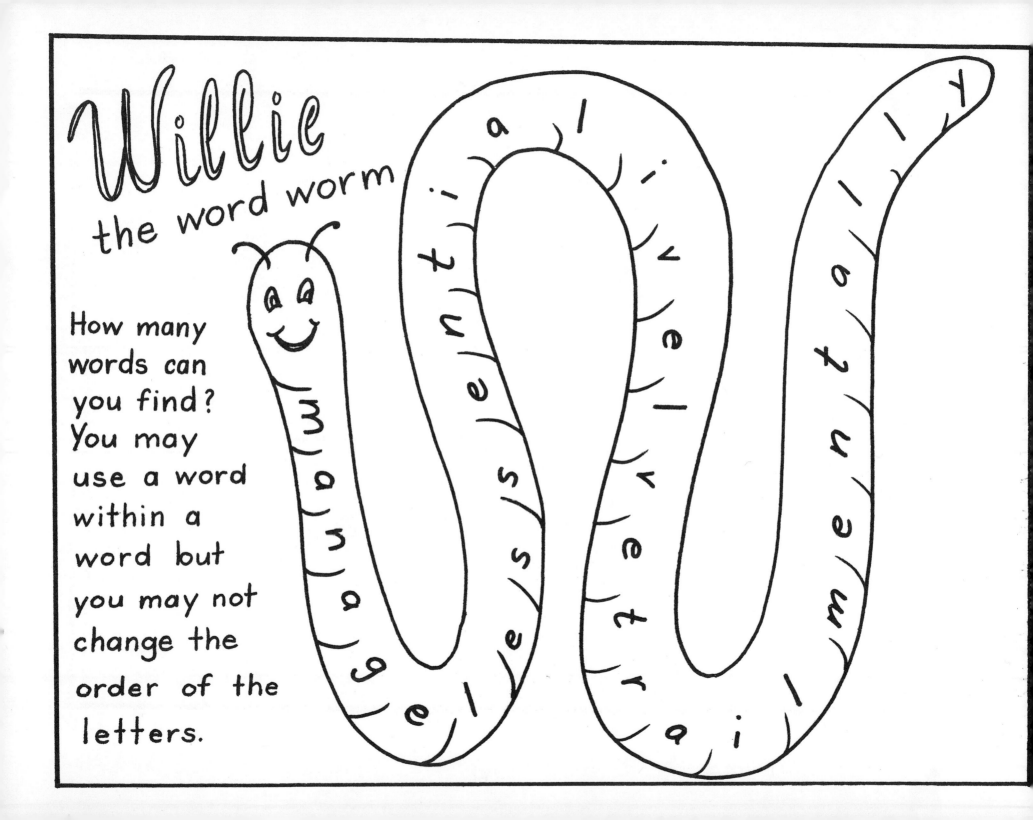

THE ZOO REVIEW

SUBJECT AREA: Writing

SKILL REINFORCED: Creative writing

ADAPTABILITY:

MATERIALS: Colored posterboard, brads, animal decals or
                     pictures, felt pens, ruler

CONSTRUCTION: Cut posterboard 12½" x 9". 3" from the outer
                     edges and 4" from the top and bottom cut a win-
                     dow 6¼" x 1". Cut 2 wheels approximately 3½"
                     in diameter. Divide in 8 equal segments. On
                     one circle write names of 8 animals and on the
                     other write 8 things that animals might do (fan-
                     tasy), for example, the lion that could dance.
                     Animals you might include are: dinosaur, gorilla,
                     tiger, giraffe, etc. Activities you might include
                     are: that went to school, that liked children,
                     that never grew up, etc. Attach the wheels 2"
                     from the outer edge and 4½" from the top.
                     Decorate.

DIRECTIONS FOR   The student spins the wheels and whatever it
PLAYING: stops on, is the subject for creative writing.

ZOO ANIMALS

The lion | | that could dance.

giraffe

lion

ger

that wo

children

who

62.

BLOOMING WORDS

SUBJECT AREA: Spelling

SKILL REINFORCED: Vocabulary development

ADAPTABILITY:

MATERIALS: Posterboard, construction paper, glue
                     felt pen, exacto knife, tagboard, scissors

CONSTRUCTION: Draw or use construction paper cutouts to
                     make outdoor scene for background on poster-
                     board. Make grass clusters from construction
                     paper and glue a piece of magnetic strip on
                     each one. Glue grass clusters on posterboard.
                     Make flowers from pastel construction paper
                     backed with pieces of magnetic strips. On
                     each flower, write a letter of the alphabet.
                     Attach flowers to grass clumps in random
                     order.

DIRECTIONS FOR   The student rearranges flowers to make words,
PLAYING: and lists each word he finds.

THE ROAD TO GOOD HEALTH

SUBJECT AREA: Science

SKILL REINFORCED: Nutritional awareness

ADAPTABILITY: Health, consumer education

MATERIALS: Heavy board or cardboard, food pictures, 1 dice, tagboard
                     construction paper, glue, felt pen, player pieces

CONSTRUCTION: Glue construction paper on game board for background, then
                     glue food pictures (may be cut from women's magazines) for
                     decoration. Finally, cut "road" from light colored construc-
                     tion paper and glue down. Mark spaces and write activity in
                     each. Make about 10 each of lunch, snack and food cards from
                     tagboard. On the food cards, paste a food picture on the
                     front, and on the back, write the food group, basic nutrients,
                     and function of that food. On the snack cards, glue pictures
                     (on the back) of foods that might be chosen for a snack and
                     assign plus values for nutritious snacks and minus values
                     for "junk" (e.g. candy bars). On the lunch cards, write
                     (on the back) a fairly typical lunch and give each food a
                     plus or minus value. Add these up and give the lunch a
                     total value.

DIRECTIONS FOR   The 1st player rolls the dice and moves his marker the number
PLAYING: of spaces rolled. He then follows directions given on the
                     space on which he lands. If he lands on a space directing
                     him to challenge an opponent to lunch, he chooses an opponent
                     and each of them draws a lunch card. The player drawing the
                     card with the highest value keeps those points. If both
                     players draw cards with minus values, they must draw again.
                     Score is kept and the player with the highest score, when
                     all players have gone around the board, wins.

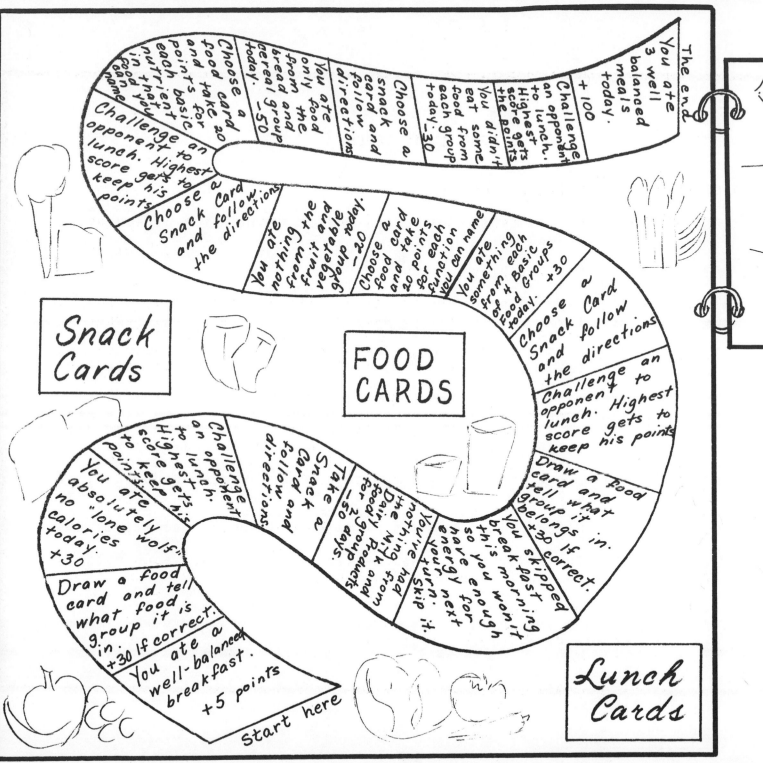

Food Cards / Snack Cards / Lunch Cards Board Game

The end

You ate 3 well balanced meals today. +100

Challenge an opponent to lunch. Highest score gets the points.

You didn't eat some food from each group today. -30

Choose a snack card and follow directions

You ate only food from the bread and cereal group today. -50

Choose a food card and take 20 points for each basic nutrient in that food you can name.

Challenge an opponent to lunch. Highest score gets to keep his points.

Choose a Snack Card and follow the directions

You ate nothing the from the fruit and vegetable group today. -20

Choose a food card and take 20 points for each function you can name +3

You ate something from each of 4 Basic Food Groups today. +30

Choose a Snack Card and follow the directions

Challenge an opponent to lunch. Highest score gets to keep his points

Draw a food card and tell what group it belongs in. +30 if correct.

You skipped breakfast this morning so you won't have enough energy for your next turn. Skip it.

You've had enough energy for your next turn. Skip it.

You ate nothing from the Milk and Dairy Group.

You ate Dairy products for breakfast. -50 days.

Take a Snack Card and follow directions.

Challenge an opponent to lunch. Highest score gets to keep his points.

You ate absolutely no "lone wolf" calories today. +30

Draw a food card and tell what food group it is in. +30 If correct.

You ate a well-balanced breakfast. +5 points

Start here

Snack Cards

FOOD CARDS

Lunch Cards

GROUP - Meat
Function-
1. Build tissue
2. Supply energy
3. Repair tissue
4. Build Antibodies
Nutrients - Iron, Protein Vitamins

FOOD CARD
(back)

Cheese Sandwich +61
Orange juice +62
Apple pie -40
TOTAL +83

LUNCH CARD
(back)

CAKE - "Lone Wolf" Calories

-30

SNACK CARD

THE MAGIC TOUCH

SUBJECT AREA: Science--ecology

SKILL REINFORCED: Environmental awareness and/or recognition of ecological groups

ADAPTABILITY: Any matching lesson

MATERIALS: Plywood or masonite (size will vary depending on how many items you intend to use on the board), drill, copper or brass nuts and bolts (must be copper or brass for good conduction), battery case and batteries*, electrical leads*, 2 volt wire*, indicator light*, receptacle for light*, cup hooks, tagboard, hole punch

CONSTRUCTION: Sketch layout of board on plywood or masonite with pencil. Make cards and labels to be matched. Punch holes in tops so these can be hung on cup hooks. This allows you to change the items to be matched. On the board, drill holes and screw in hooks for cards. Below each card, drill hole and screw in bolt. Attach leads and batteries to back of board. Mount receptacle for light bulb at top of board. Attach wires to nuts of matching items. See illustration.

DIRECTIONS FOR   The student touches one lead to bolt under each matching
PLAYING: item. If correct, light goes on.

*These are available at electronics stores.

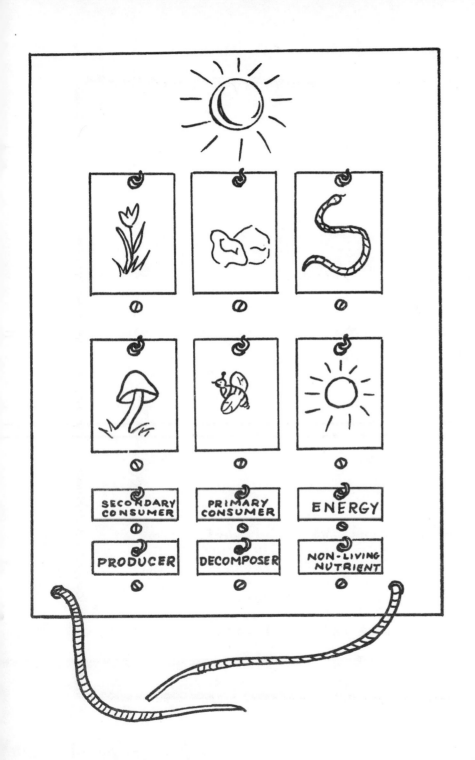

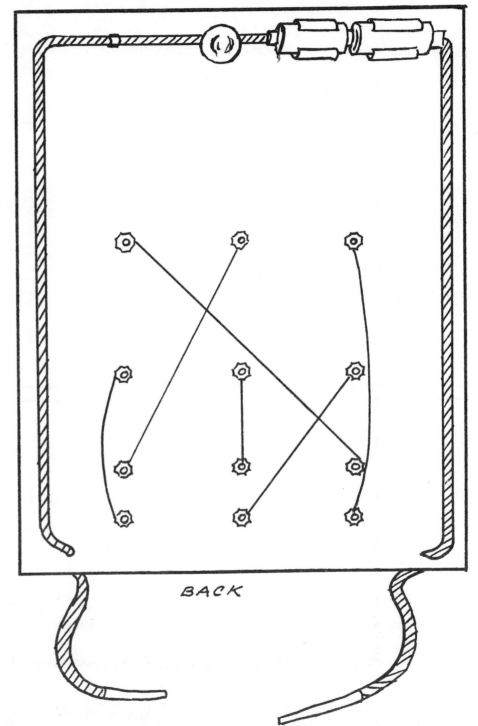

BACK

68.

SOLUTION TO POLLUTION

SUBJECT AREA: Science--ecology

SKILL REINFORCED: Environmental awareness

ADAPTABILITY: Science, reading, math, civil procedure, civic
                     responsibility

MATERIALS: Old gameboard, heavy posterboard, or cardboard,
                     felt pens, posterboard in contrasting color,
                     one dice, player pieces (buttons, cardboard
                     squares, etc.), score card or sheet for each
                     player

CONSTRUCTION: Make board as illustrated. Then cut cards to
                     represent the Grocery, Legislature, and Voter
                     cards.

                     The Grocery Cards should read:

                         You bought detergent with phosphates. -6
                         You bought Snax-Pax cereals with all that
                             extra wrapping. -3
                         You bought plastic garbage bags instead of
                             paper. -3
                         You bought white toilet tissue instead of
                             colored. +3
                         You bought a no-phosphate detergent. +5

CONSTRUCTION: You bought soft drinks in returnable
(continued)   bottles. +5
                  You bought soft drinks in aluminum cans
                     and recycled them. +7
                  You bought an insecticide for your roses
                     which contained a harmful pollutant. -3

The Legislature Cards should read:

   That's a great idea. We pass it--on to
      the voters. +1
   Good idea. Take it to the voters. +2
   We approve. Take it to the voters. +3
   Big business would be against such an idea
      and we have to think about those cam-
      paign contributions. No. -2
   Good idea, but too expensive. No. -3
   It's a great idea but the people on the
      north side of town are bound to oppose--
      and that's a lot of votes. No. -4

The Voter Cards should read:

   Not worth our tax dollars. No.-2
   A ½% tax increase?!! No way! -3
   This sounds expensive. No. -3
   Sounds like a real asset to our community.
      Yes. +10
   Passed! +10
   Since big business will be footing the bill,
      we approve. +10

DIRECTIONS FOR
PLAYING:

This game may be played by 2 to 6 children.
The dice is rolled by each and the one who
rolls the highest number begins the play.
He rolls again and moves his playing piece
the proper number of spaces on the board.
If the space on which he lands has a plus or
minus value, he records it on his score card.
If the space has instructions to go to the
grocery or the legislature, he draws an
appropriate card. Each grocery card has a
plus or minus value which he records on his
score card. The legislature card may carry
a minus value or it may carry a plus value
and instructions to go on to the voters. If
instructed to do so, he draws a voter card
and records this value on his score card.
The person on his left then plays. As a
player nears the end of the board, he may
roll the exact number or any higher number to
reach the end of the board. The game is over
when every player has moved around the board.
The player having the highest score wins.

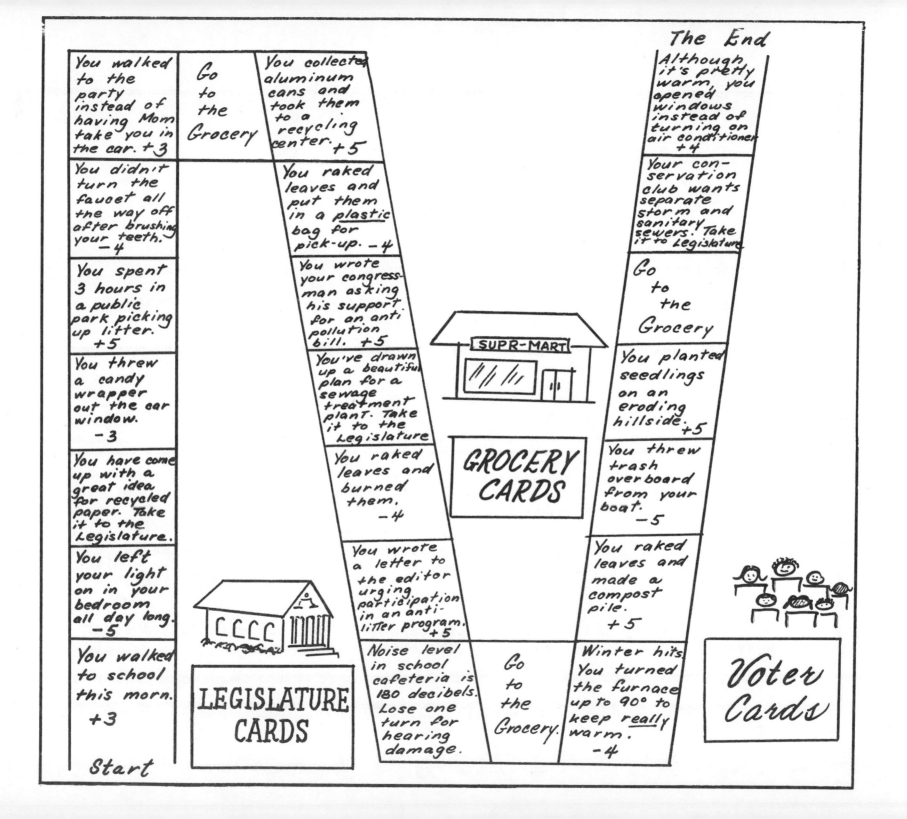

THE KNOW-IT-ALL

SUBJECT AREA: Math

SKILL REINFORCED: Multiplication facts

ADAPTABILITY: Any kind of drill involving question and answer

MATERIALS: ½ gallon milk carton, exacto knife, contact paper, railroad board or posterboard

CONSTRUCTION: Open top of milk carton completely. Cover the milk carton with contact paper. Make a slit 1 3/4" from the top where the milk carton bends. Make a slit 1 3/4" from the bottom. Make each slit about ¼" in width. Cut railroad board about 13½" x 3¼". Taper the board at one end so it fits in the slit. Place the board in the milk carton, running one end through the bottom slit. Close the top of the carton by stapling the top of the board flush with the top of the carton. The railroad board should be taut before taping it on the bottom of the carton.

Cut cards so they will fit into the slit. Write the multiplication problem on the front. Write answer on back, upside down to lettering on front. Make a black dot or some kind of notation to show which side should be up and which end should go in first.

DIRECTIONS FOR PLAYING: The student puts card into computer with dotted side up and checks the answer accordingly.

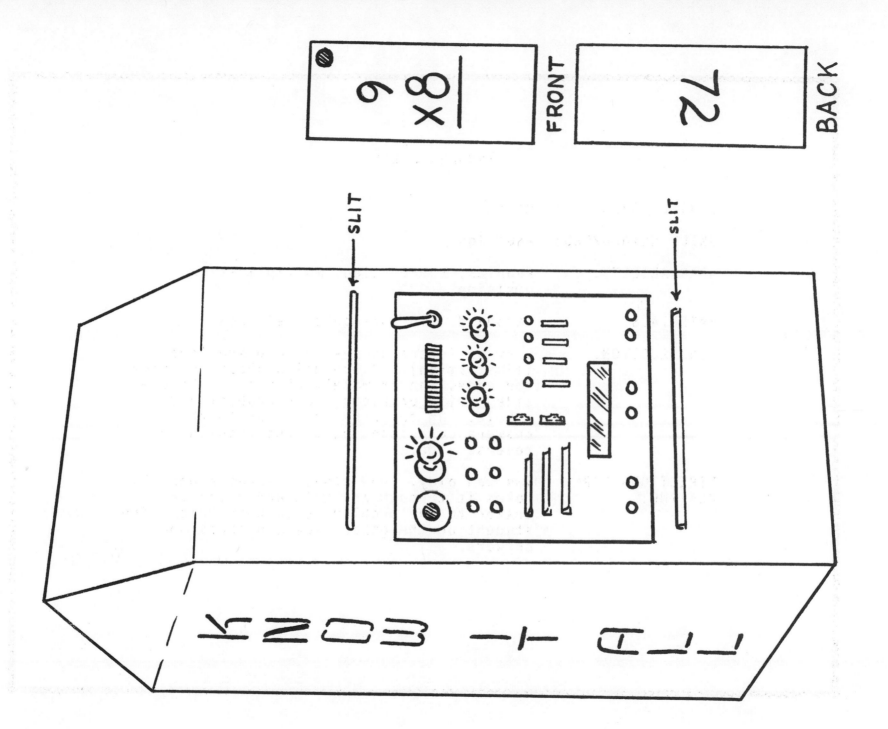

FRONT

9
x8
___

BACK

72

SLIT

SLIT

LOGIC TI BOX

ANSWER HOLES

SUBJECT AREA: Math

SKILL REINFORCED: Addition

ADAPTABILITY: Phonics, subtraction, multiplication,
                    division

MATERIALS: Tagboard, old workbooks, felt pens

CONSTRUCTION: Draw different shapes on tagboard (see
                    illustration). Punch holes about 1½" from
                    the edge, approximately 2" apart. On one
                    side, write problems, each problem above
                    a hole. On the other side, write the
                    answers corresponding to the problems on
                    reverse side.

DIRECTIONS FOR   Two can play. One student takes a pencil,
PLAYING: pokes it through any hole and gives the
                    answer to the problem above that hole. The
                    student on the other side can check the
                    answers.

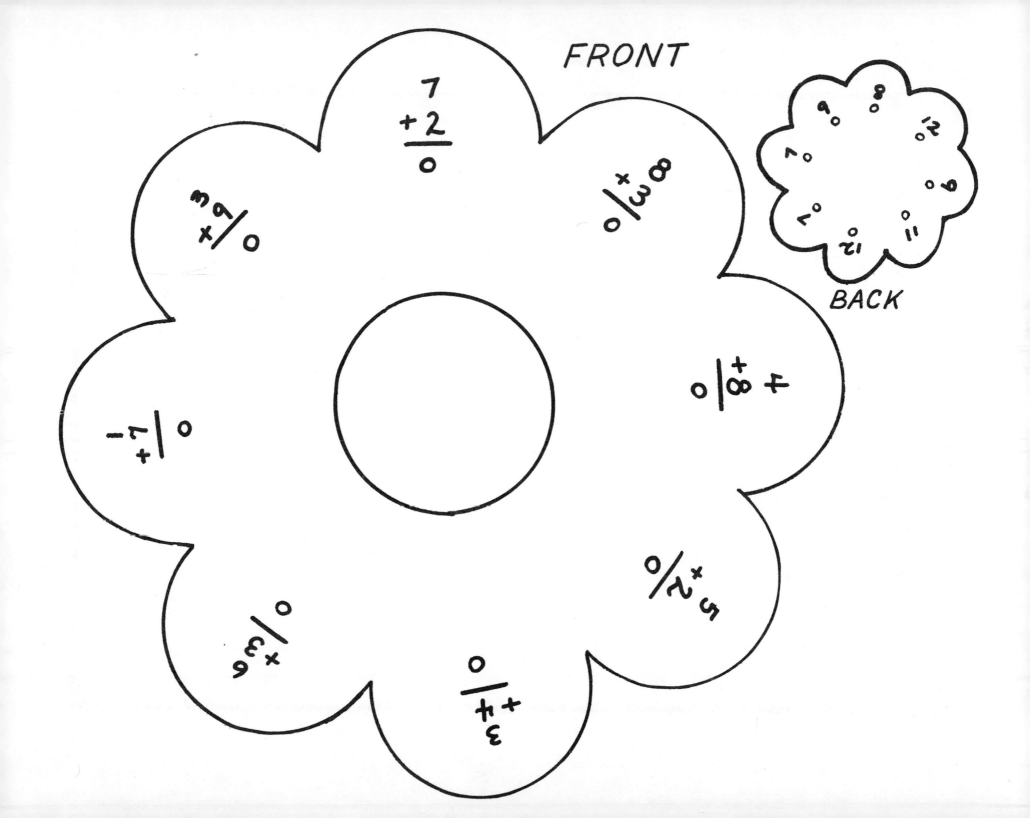

MULTIPLY YOUR CONCENTRATION

SUBJECT AREA: Math

SKILL REINFORCED: Multiplication

ADAPTABILITY: Math combinations, phonics, vocabulary

MATERIALS: Two cardboard pieces 13½" x 17½", exacto knife, solid color contact paper, tagboard, felt pens

CONSTRUCTION: Cover one side of both cardboard pieces with contact paper. Then cut 20 windows in one of the cardboard pieces. The windows should measure approximately 2" x 3½" each, four windows across and five down. The windows are ½" from the edge and 1" between them. Glue the cut-out cardboard onto the other board. Cut tagboard into 20 2" x 3" pieces. Write multiplication facts on 10 of the cards. Write the answers to those facts on the other ten.

DIRECTIONS FOR PLAYING: Two or more can play. Cards are turned face down on the board. The first player turns a card over and gives the answer. If the answer is correct, a second card is turned up. If that card is the answer to the first card turned up, the player gets to keep both cards. If an incorrect answer is given to the first card turned over, the player does not get to turn over a second card. The one with the most cards, when all cards are taken, wins.

6 X 2			
		12	

TEA TIMES

SUBJECT AREA: Math

SKILL REINFORCED: Multiplication

ADAPTABILITY: Basic math facts, phonics, word recognition, synonyms, antonyms, homonyms

MATERIALS: Old gameboard or heavy cardboard, construction paper, felt pens, magnetic strip, scissors, glue

CONSTRUCTION: Draw a dining room table big enough for a number of cups and saucers. Cut cups and saucers. Write matching items on cups and saucers. Cut magnetic strips and place them on the table where the cups and saucers would be placed. Then place a piece of magnetic strip on the back and front of the saucer, and back of the cup. Answers may be written on the back of each cup.

DIRECTIONS FOR PLAYING: Student matches the items by placing the correct cup on each saucer.

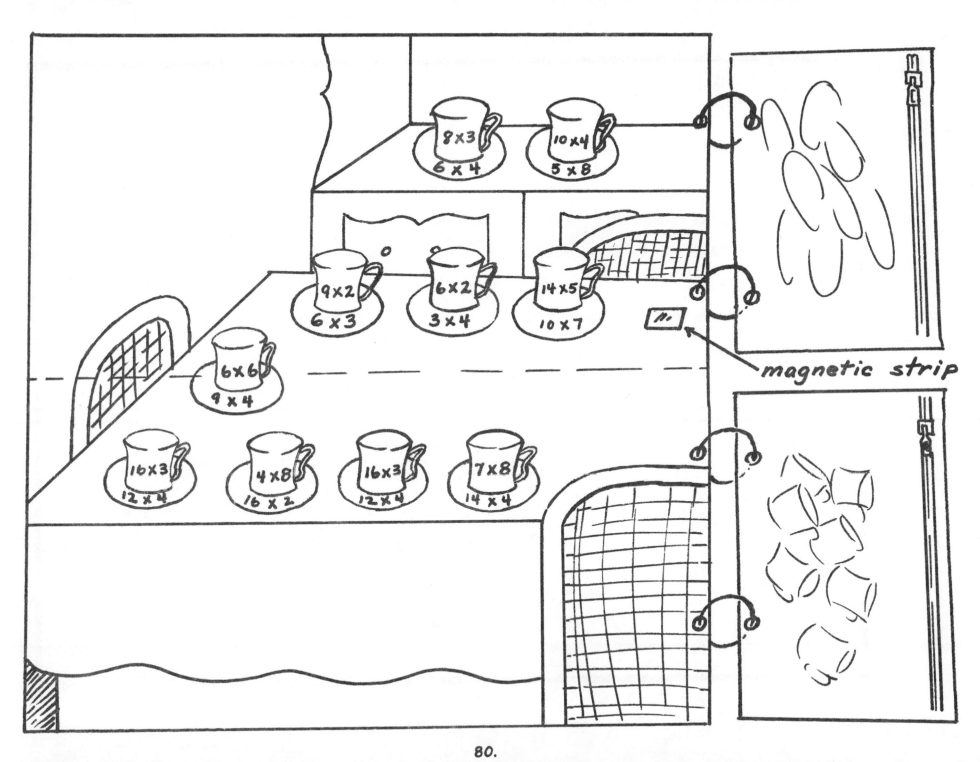

magnetic strip

STAND UP AND COUNT

SUBJECT AREA: Math

SKILL REINFORCED: Expanded notation

ADAPTABILITY: Vocabulary, spelling, color recognition

MATERIALS: Thick cardboard, preferably Tri-Wall, tagboard,
                     felt pens, glue

CONSTRUCTION: Cut cardboard or Tri-Wall into the following
                     pieces: 1 15" x 4"; 1 15 x 3"; 1 15 x 2".
                     Cover these with contact paper. Glue the
                     15" x 2" flush with one end of the 15" x 4"
                     piece. Glue the 15" x 3" about ¼" apart from
                     the 15" x 2", thus making a stand. Cut 3" x 4"
                     cards. On each of them mark the top with a
                     numeral and write the expanded notation on the
                     bottom of the card. On the back, you may want
                     to reverse the process: write the expanded
                     notation on top and the numeral on the bottom.
                     Then make 3" square cards to correspond with the
                     3" x 4" cards. On these, write the numerals on
                     one side and expanded notation on the other.

DIRECTIONS FOR   The student places his cards in the stand and
PLAYING: matches the smaller cards to them. Then he
                     lifts up his card to see if it is right. Only
                     when the card is lifted can the answer be seen.

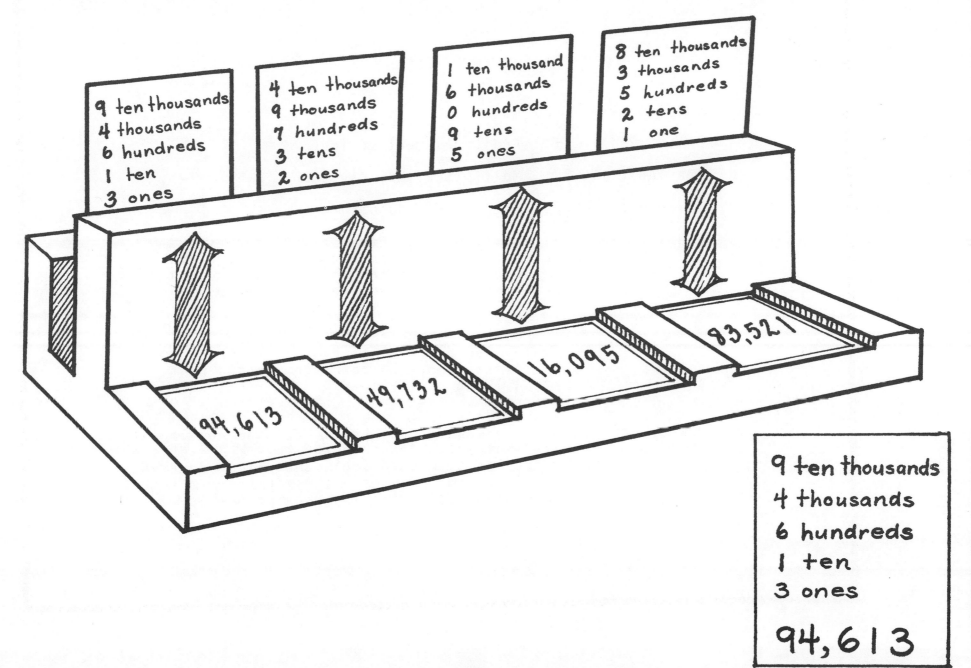

9 ten thousands
4 thousands
6 hundreds
1 ten
3 ones

4 ten thousands
9 thousands
7 hundreds
3 tens
2 ones

1 ten thousand
6 thousands
0 hundreds
9 tens
5 ones

8 ten thousands
3 thousands
5 hundreds
2 tens
1 one

94,613

79,732

16,095

83,521

9 ten thousands
4 thousands
6 hundreds
1 ten
3 ones

94,613

FUNNY FACE

SUBJECT AREA: Math

SKILLS REINFORCED: Addition, subtraction

ADAPTABILITY: Multiplication, division

MATERIALS: Felt pens, tagboard

CONSTRUCTION: Cut tagboard into 5" x 5" squares. Any
                       kind of a decorative drawing or decal
                       can be put in the middle, just to get
                       away from the monotony of numbers. Rule
                       off 7 lines or more on each side. Write
                       numbers at random on the left. If the
                       concept being taught is +2 and the first
                       number on the left side is 4, then the
                       first number on the right should be 6.
                       All the other lines on the right should
                       remain blank.

DIRECTIONS FOR   The student chooses a card and, by looking
PLAYING: at the top lines on the left and right,
                       tries to figure the mathematical function
                       involved. He then fills in the remaining
                       blanks following the same principle.

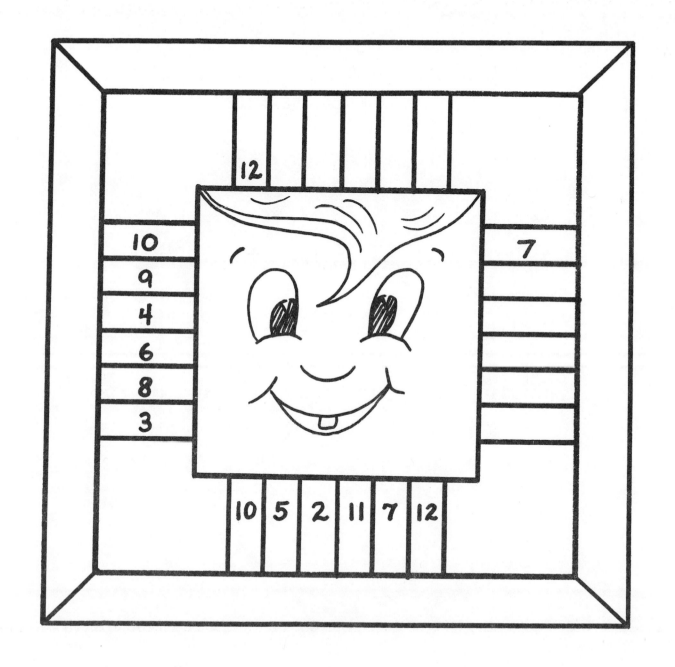

84.

FIDDLE-DE-BEADS

SUBJECT AREA: Math

SKILL REINFORCED: Addition

ADAPTABILITY: Counting, subtraction

MATERIALS: Felt pens, posterboard, shoe laces, small
                     wooden beads

CONSTRUCTION: Write addition problems on one side of
                     posterboard. On the other, illustrate
                     the answer with circles. On the bottom
                     of card, punch hole and tie shoe laces.

DIRECTIONS FOR   The student takes a card, computes the
PLAYING: addition by threading the right number
                     of beads on the shoe lace. He can check
                     back of card for the right number of
                     beads.

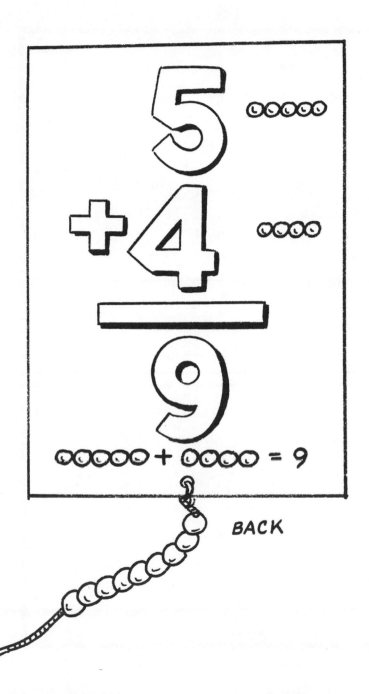

BACK

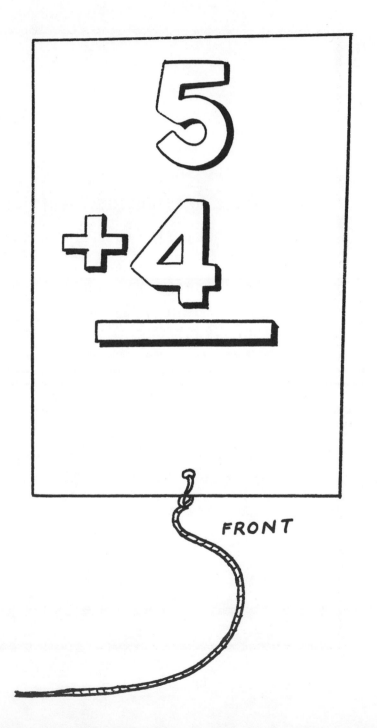

FRONT

86.

MAKE YOUR OWN PUZZLE

SUBJECT AREA: Math

SKILL REINFORCED: Division

ADAPTABILITY: Math combinations, parts of speech, phonics,
                     fractions

MATERIALS: An appealing picture, preferably one with nothing
                     printed on the back, scissors, felt pens, tagboard

CONSTRUCTION: Cut the picture into basically the same shapes,
                     making sure the pieces do not get mixed (other-
                     wise you might be spending a lot of time putting
                     them back together again!). Draw an outline of
                     each shape on the tagboard. Write matching items
                     on each puzzle piece and its corresponding shape
                     on the board.

DIRECTIONS FOR   The student tries to put the picture together
PLAYING: by matching the items.

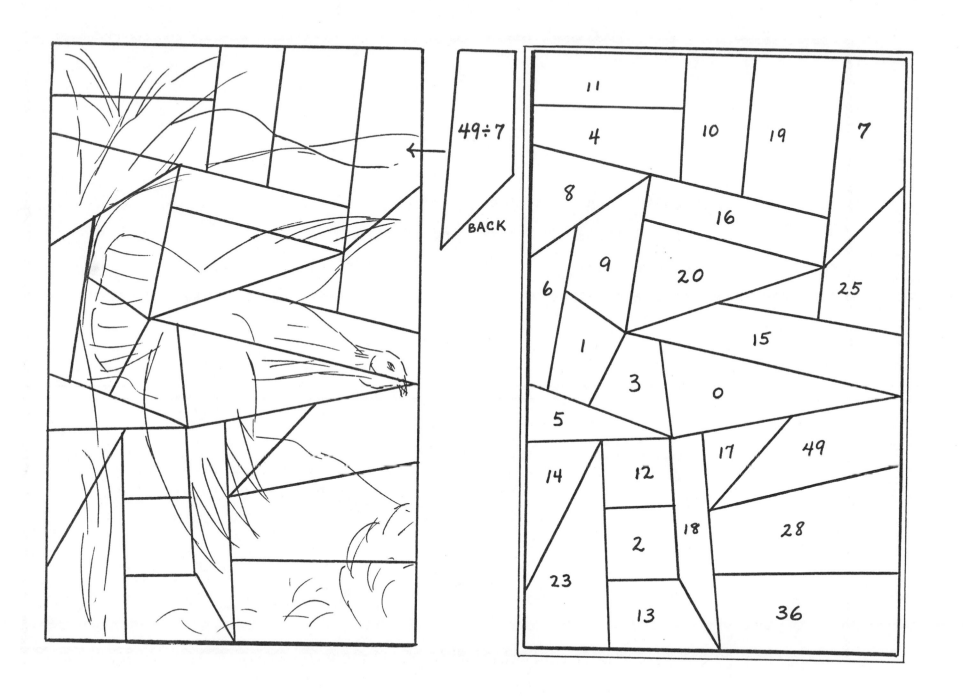

$49 \div 7$

BACK

DUMP THE DICE

SUBJECT AREA:	Math
SKILL REINFORCED:	Beginning addition
ADAPTABILITY:	Alphabet, subtraction, multiplication
MATERIALS:	4 8" square boxes (they can be obtained from the post office), felt, scissors, glue
CONSTRUCTION:	Cover boxes with felt. Cut 5" numerals 1-12 and glue on each side of box. On the other two boxes glue circles to correspond with the numerals (they will look like big dice).
DIRECTIONS FOR PLAYING:	Four people can play. Throw the two that have the numerals. Add. Then find corresponding dice and count circles to see if the answer is correct.

KLIP THE KLOCK

SUBJECT AREA: Math

SKILL REINFORCED: Multiplication

ADAPTABILITY: Phonics, math combinations

MATERIALS: Cardboard, plain contact paper, felt
                      markers, clothes pins

CONSTRUCTION: Cut cardboard approximately 7½" x 10".
                      Divide into as many parts as desired.
                      Write multiplication problems on the
                      cardboard and the matching answers on the
                      back. Then write answers on the clothes
                      pins with felt pens.

DIRECTIONS FOR   Student clips the clothes pin to the card-
PLAYING: board, with answer facing down. After the
                      student has clipped all of them the answers
                      can be checked. The answer on the clothes
                      pin should be in the same place as the
                      answer on the back of the cardboard.

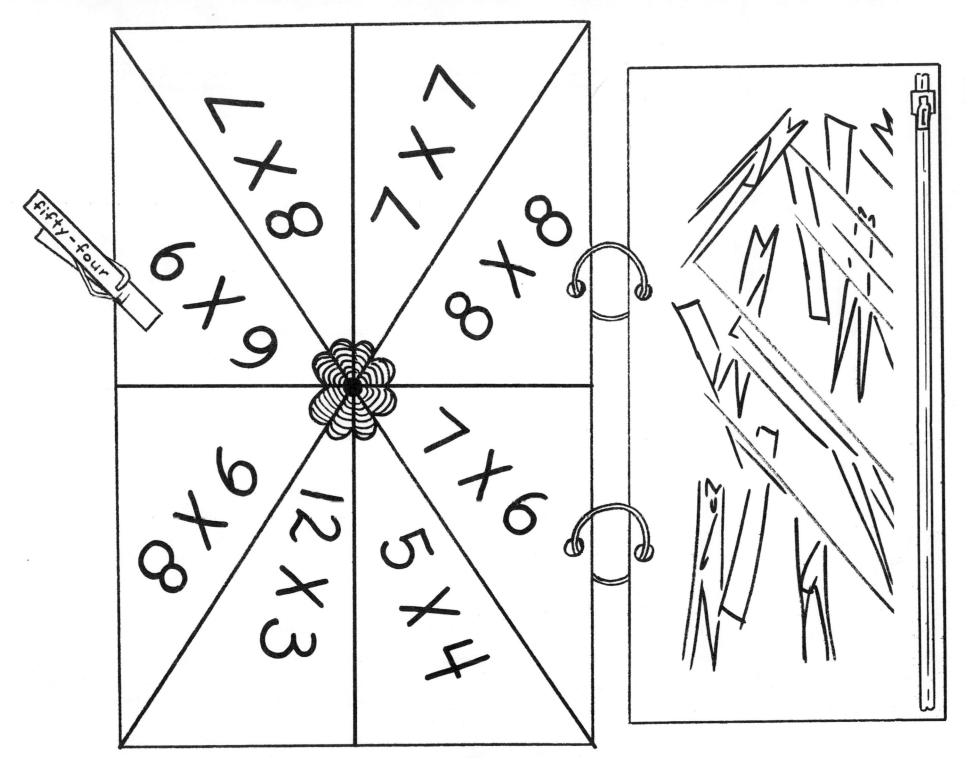

fifty-four

7 X 7

7 X 8

8 X 8

6 X 9

7 X 6

8 X 6

5 X 4

12 X 3

FLIP AND FIGURE

SUBJECT AREA: Math

SKILL REINFORCED: Word problems involving money

ADAPTABILITY: Any area of matn involving word or story problems

MATERIALS: Felt pens, notebook rings, tagboard, small pictures
                       (optional), hole punch

CONSTRUCTION: Cut 2 pieces of tagboard 12" x 5" for covers. Make
                       4 word problems with 3 parts each. The problems
                       must be planned so that the parts can be interchanged.
                       Cut 12 cards 3 3/4" x 4 3/4" from tagboard. Write
                       each part of each problem on a separate card. Punch
                       2 holes in the left side of each card. Put all of
                       the part 1 cards in a stack and attach them to the
                       covers at the top (see illustration). Below them,
                       attach the part 2 cards and, below them, the part 3
                       cards. On the front cover write "Mrs. Spendthrift's
                       Shopping Spree" and decorate with appropriate pictures
                       cut from magazines, if desired. On the inside back
                       cover make an answer code. This can be done by
                       coding the part 1 cards 1,2,3, and 4, the part 2 cards
                       A,B,C, and D and the part 3 cards □ , △ , ★ , ◇ and
                       the answers can be listed 1,C,□ = 6, etc.

DIRECTIONS FOR   The student flips the cards, works the problem and
PLAYING: checks the answer.

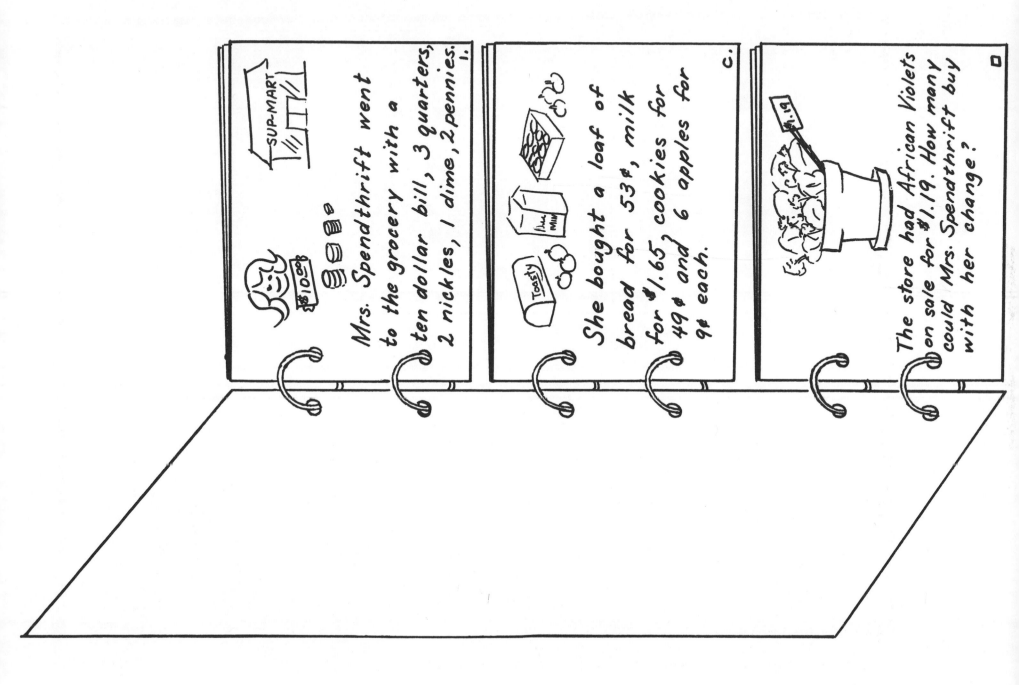

1. Mrs. Spendthrift went to the grocery with a ten dollar bill, 3 quarters, 2 nickles, 1 dime, 2 pennies.

$10.00 SUP-MART

c. She bought a loaf of bread for 53¢, milk for $1.65, cookies for 49¢ and 6 apples for 9¢ each.

Toasty

□ The store had African Violets on sale for $1.19. How many could Mrs. Spendthrift buy with her change?

$1.19

COMPUTERIZED CHOICES

SUBJECT AREA: Math

SKILL REINFORCED: Multiplication

ADAPTABILITY: Math combinations, parts of speech, phonics, homonyms,
                     synonyms, antonyms, phonics, alphabet

MATERIALS: 2 wood strips 8" x 1"
                     2 wood strips 12" x 3/4"
                     1 wood strip 6" x 1"
                     1 wood strip 4½" x 3/4"
                     1 piece plywood 12" x 14"
                     1 piece pegboard 12" x 6"
                     1 piece masonite (or more) 12" x 4¼"
                     Tagboard 8" x 10"
                     Newsprint 11 3/4" x 4"
                     Glue, felt pens, ruler, drill

CONSTRUCTION: (Illustration, step 1): Glue the 2 8" x 1" wood strips
                        flush with the left side of the plywood, one on top
                        and the other on the bottom.
                     (Illustration, step 2): Where these two wood strips
                        end, glue one 12" x 3/4" wood strip.
                     (Illustration, step 3): Flush with the right side of
                        the plywood piece, glue the other 12" x 3/4" strip.
                        Glue the 4½" x 3/4" strip flush with the bottom between
                        the 12" strips.
                     (Illustration, step 4): On top of the two 12" x 3/4"
                        strips glue the piece of pegboard.
                     (Illustration, step 5): Flush with the top of the peg-
                        board, glue the 6" x 1" strip. On the short strip
                        write 1 through 4 directly above the rows of holes.

Cut tagboard 8" x 10". Rule 10 lines 1" apart. 4" from
the left make 4 lines 1" apart lengthwise. On the left
write the problems. In the four spaces on the right give
four choices of answers, with only one being the right
answer for each line. Depending on the number of problems (tagboard sheets) you have, you need the corresponding number of answer boards (masonite).

Place tagboard sheet on computer board (left side--should
fit exactly!). Slide the masonite from the top through the
slit in the computer board all the way to the bottom.
Directly above the tagboard, in line with the rows, mark 1
through 4. Now if your correct answer to problem 1 is
answer 3, poke pencil through pegboard hole number 3 and
mark it heavily. Do the same with the rest of the cards.
After all the masonite boards are marked (it must be accu-
rate) drill holes in the masonite. The answer board (masonite) and card (tagboard) must be coded the same way so
students know which two go together.

DIRECTIONS FOR
PLAYING:
The student takes a card, corresponding answer board and a
piece of paper (newsprint or similar paper). The card is
then placed on the computer board. He places the paper on
top of the answer board and slides both through the top of
the computer board on the right. For each row, the student
selects an answer. If he selects answer 3, he punches the
hole with a pencil under number 3 for that row. If the
answer is right, the pencil will poke through, making a
hole in the answer sheet, but if it is wrong, the pencil
will hit the masonite.

X-3		1	2	3	4
2 X 3		6	8	10	4
2 X 5		8	12	10	14
2 X 10		26	20	22	24
2 X 8		22	20	18	16
2 X 4		14	8	10	12
2 X 0		4	8	0	2
2 X 9		14	16	18	20
2 X 2		10	4	6	8
2 X 11		28	22	24	26
2 X 1		4	2	6	8
2 X 12		20	28	22	24
2 X 7		12	16	14	18

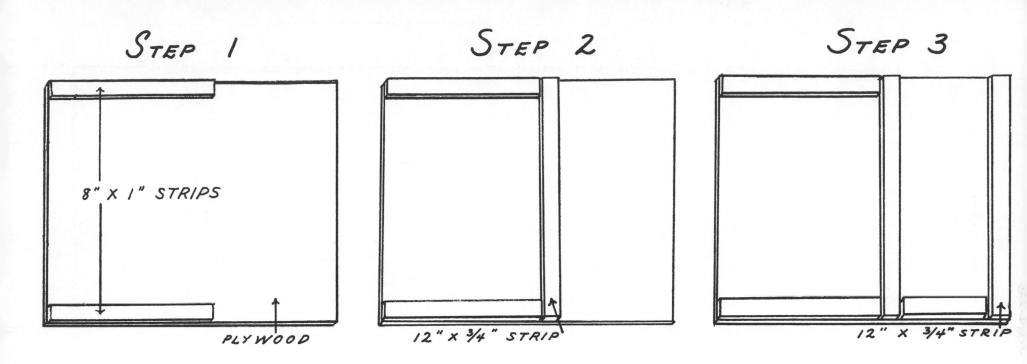

Step 1

8" X 1" STRIPS

PLYWOOD

Step 2

12" X ¾" STRIP

Step 3

12" X ¾" STRIP

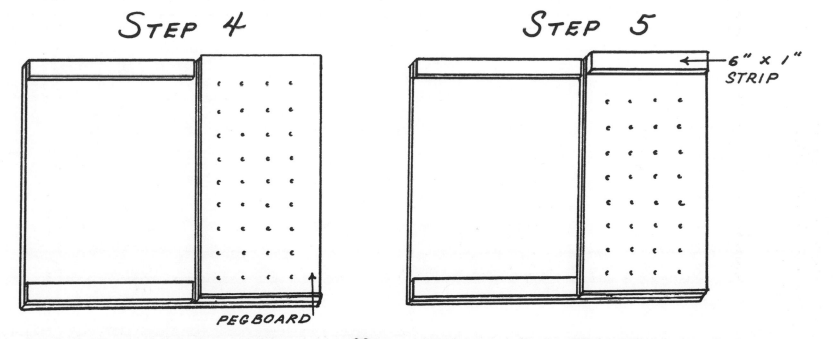

Step 4

PEGBOARD

Step 5

6" X 1" STRIP

PLACE VALUE BEADS

SUBJECT AREA: Math

SKILL REINFORCED: Place value recognition

ADAPTABILITY:

MATERIALS: Tagboard, felt pens, beads (preferably in six
                       different colors), heavy twine, hole punch

CONSTRUCTION: Cut tagboard into rectangles about 4½" x 5½".
                       About ¼" from the bottom, punch six holes--the
                       first 3/8" from the edge and at 3/4" intervals
                       after that. On the front of the card above the
                       first hole on the left write 100,000, above the
                       next hole 10,000, then 1,000, then 100, then 10,
                       and finally 1. Tie a piece of heavy twine
                       through each hole leaving about 6" hanging.
                       Next, write a 6 digit number in the middle of
                       the card. On the back draw circles to represent
                       beads for each place value. Reverse the numbers
                       so that the same string represents the one on
                       the back as the front (see illustration).

DIRECTIONS FOR   The student uses beads to illustrate place value
PLAYING: by stringing the appropriate number of beads
                       under each value. He then turns card over to
                       check his work.

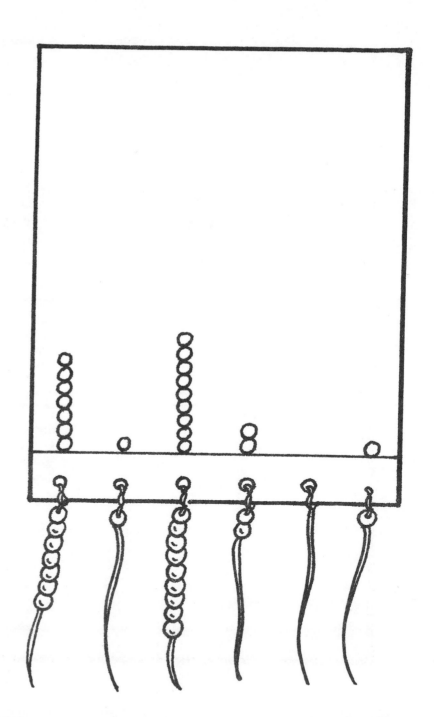

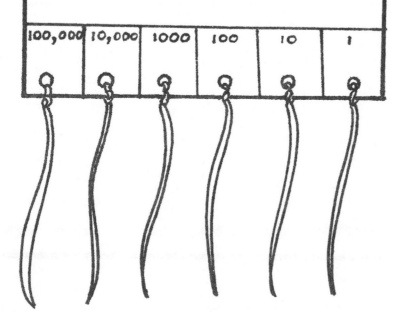

100,000	10,000	1000	100	10	1

FOOLING WITH FROGS

SUBJECT AREA: Math

SKILLS REINFORCED: Recognition of number words and numerals

ADAPTABILITY:

MATERIALS: Construction paper, felt pens, scissors

CONSTRUCTION: Make 10 or more frogs out of construction
                       paper. Write the numeral on the left
                       side, matching number word on the right
                       side and the set on the bottom. Cut
                       each frog into three pieces as illustrated.

DIRECTIONS FOR   The student matches the number word,
PLAYING: numeral, and set. If correctly matched,
                       it will make a frog.

CUT

SCARVING THE SNOWMEN

SUBJECT AREA: Math

SKILL REINFORCED: Addition

ADAPTABILITY: Expanded notation, synonyms, homonyms, math
                     combinations, color discrimination, etc.

MATERIALS: Old gameboard or heavy cardboard, construc-
                     tion paper, felt pens, magnetic strip, scissors

CONSTRUCTION: Draw a snow scene for background. Glue on game-
                     board. Cut snowmen (approximately 20). Use
                     colors other than black for the hat. Glue snowmen
                     on the board. Do not glue the scarves. Write
                     matching items on the hats and scarves. Do not
                     use matching colors for the hats and scarves
                     except for color discrimination game. Put
                     magnetic strips on the back of the scarves as
                     well as on the necks of the snowmen.

DIRECTIONS FOR   The student matches the item on the scarf with
PLAYING: the one on the hat.

magnetic strip

9+10
front

19
back

magnetic strip

104.

Helpful Hints

Listed below are a few ideas that have proved helpful to us:

1. It is helpful to the children if parts of the game are kept together with the gameboard. The authors have purchased zippered plastic bags that have served this purpose well. You will note that most of the games illustrated have a plastic bag attached.

2. Games need to be attractive (use lots of contrasting colors) as well as durable. We suggest laminating all the games and their parts. However, if laminating film is not available, clear contact paper makes a good substitute.

3. Suction spinners are handy. They can be used with any type of game that requires a spinner. Some school supply stores carry these.

4. After a game is laminated, only permanent felt tip markers will write on it. Two brands we have had success with are:

    Broad tip: El Marko permanent marker by Flair
    Thin point: Sanford's Sharpie

5. Games that are made attractively should be displayed where they catch the attention of the children. We suggest game racks similar to the display shelves found in card shops, grocery stores, liquor stores, etc.

6. Do not let a lack of artistic ability discourage you from trying these activities. We have found parents to be a rich resource. They are often very capable and willing to copy and assemble games. This does not necessarily have to be accomplished by one parent in one day but may involve several parents for a prolonged period of time.

7. Old gameboards can often be adapted for many of these games. The children are usually very happy to contribute them.

8. We have found it helpful to have several copies of many of these games because often a group of children are working simultaneously on the same skill.

INDEX